FADE TO ZILCH

FADE TO ZILCH

A SCREENPLAY

BY F. LEWIS HALL

BASED ON THE NOVEL THE UNBEARABLE SADNESS OF ZILCH
BY KONRAD VENTANA

TRUE DIRECTIONS | iUniverse®
AN AFFILIATE OF TARCHER BOOKS

FADE TO ZILCH
A SCREENPLAY

This is a work of fiction. All of the characters, names, incidents, organizations, and dialogue in this novel are either the products of the author's imagination or are used fictitiously.

iUniverse books may be ordered through booksellers or by contacting:

iUniverse
1663 Liberty Drive
Bloomington, IN 47403
www.iuniverse.com
1-800-Authors (1-800-288-4677)

ISBN: 978-1-4917-6466-4 (sc)
ISBN: 978-1-4917-6465-7 (hc)
ISBN: 978-1-4917-6464-0 (e)

Library of Congress Control Number: 2015905091

Print information available on the last page.

iUniverse rev. date: 4/27/2015

FADE IN:

EXT. LOS ANGELES BASIN (AERIAL) - DAY

We're FLYING NORTH above a receding layer of maritime clouds, skirting the Pacific COASTLINE, approaching that huge bowl of sediment and sand that is the Los Angeles Basin. ANGLE ON - The COASTAL PLAIN, DESCENDING SLOWLY between the Palos Verdes Peninsula and the Transverse Range of Santa Monica Mountains, thinly covered with patches of fog and green. The Los Angeles SKYLINE comes prominently into view.

> NARRATOR, METROS (V.O.)
> No one is innocent … not in this town. In this town, the apocalypse has come and gone, lifting the veil of innocence like a great velvet curtain in an old movie house, where the only victims that don't return for the sequel are the gods themselves, struck out long ago by the big blue pencil …

ANGLE ON - DOWNTOWN LA, shimmering in the morning sun.

> NARRATOR, METROS (V.O.) (CONT'D)
> In this town, every man, woman, and child takes the limits of his or her own field of vision to be the limits of the world …

We're ANGLING toward the COAST again, overlooking the foggy veil of Malibu, the Palisades, and the Santa Monica Mountains, where STYLISH HOMES are seen peppering the hilly landscapes.

> NARRATOR, METROS (V.O.) (CONT'D)
> Without the lamplights of fate that flicker in a constant state of anxiety through yonder movie reels, the collective vision would be blacker than the slate of a director's clapboard.

We're FLYING LOWER now, ARCING INLAND over Beverly Hills toward Hollywood Hills. ANGLE ON - UNIVERSAL CITYWALK, crawling with flocks of tourists.

> NARRATOR, METROS (V.O.) (CONT'D)
> No one is pure … not in this town. Sadly, that immortal
> instinct that senses the beautiful as it aspires to the divine
> is viewed nowadays as the desire of the moth for the star …

ANGLE ON - the iconic HOLLYWOOD SIGN, which is literally DRIPPING with bloodred STAGE PAINT. CLOSE ON - we see the SCAFFOLDS and BOOMS and a team of PAINTERS busily returning the "bloodstained" letters to a pristine state of whiteness.

> NARRATOR, METROS (V.O.) (CONT'D)
> In this town, the boundaries that separate real life from
> mere living death are, at best, shadowy and vague. No
> longer is there any wild effort to reach that elusive beauty
> above, only a cool satisfaction with the garish beauty that
> is flashed before us.

We're DESCENDING SLOWLY, ANGLE ON - STREET SIGN "Hollywood Blvd.," throngs of tourists traipsing over the WALK OF FAME. ANGLE ON - SIGN "Sunset Blvd.," then on to the SUNSET STRIP, congested with traffic. CLOSE ON - a flatbed TOW TRUCK bearing an ASTON MARTIN DB9 coupe, which we FOLLOW along Western Avenue and Los Feliz Boulevard, Hollywood, to a seedy, whitewashed OFFICE BUILDING.

> NARRATOR, METROS (V.O.) (CONT'D)
> Some might call me cynical -- but I'm a philosophical
> counselor, not a cynic. I do not carry a lantern in the
> daytime, nor am I looking for an honest man -- just a
> paying client with the weight of the world on his shoulders.

ANGLE ON - The flatbed TOW TRUCK pulls up outside the seedy OFFICE BUILDING, and the REPO MAN proceeds, methodically, to off-load the DB9 coupe. FOCUS ON - A SHARP-DRESSED MAN (ZILCH), who STORMS BY and then ENTERS the seedy three-story OFFICE BUILDING.

> NARRATOR, METROS (V.O.) (CONT'D)
> From the lonely captain of industry, to the aging starlet,
> to the gambler who is plumb out of luck, philosophical

counselors like me are time-honored physicians of a troubled culture. We offer applied philosophy as a medicine to ease the suffering of our clients, who, <u>like this sharp-dressed man here</u>, are experiencing very serious distress.

The LONG SHOT, which started high in the sky and then moved to the Repo Man depositing his load, now moves up to an OPEN WINDOW of the seedy OFFICE BUILDING and then THROUGH the OPEN WINDOW, seemingly inside the room, becoming an EXT.-to-INT. SHOT.

INT. METROS'S OUTER OFFICE - DAY

Zilch (robust, middle-aged, dapper, intense, headstrong) READS ALOUD the NAME and the TITLE stenciled in GOLD LETTERS on the outer DOOR of the office.

> ZILCH
> (brusquely, out loud)
> "Dr. Joseph Metropolis, PhD, LPC,
> Philosophical Counselor! No Shit!"

The MAN BARGES IN, passes rudely by an attractive SECRETARY with a practiced "talk-to-the-hand" gesture, enters the INNER OFFICE, where Dr. Joseph Metropolis is seated at his desk, and SLAMS the door behind him.

> ZILCH (CONT'D)
> You must be Joe Metropolis. I'm Zero Vaynilovich, and I
> need to speak with you immediately, if not sooner.

Without offering his hand or waiting for an invitation, the impatient man pulls up a nearby armchair and seats himself. Dr. Joseph Metropolis, METROS (in his late thirties, handsome, professional, academic, and yet fashionable) offers the man a seat.

> METROS
> Please have a seat, Mr. Vaynilovich. What can I do for you
> today?

You can call me <u>Zilch</u> for starters, and don't get smart with me; I eat guys like you for breakfast. I'm here because I want you to do something for me ... something personal.

METROS

Go on.

ZILCH

I'm a very important man in this town. Several thousand people are on my payroll. And when I snap, they jump so quickly they don't even think first!

FREEZE-FRAME, ANGLE ON - Zilch, focusing on his facial expression: that dull glimmer of helplessness that stands defiantly in the furrows between the blackness of his pupils and the dull metallic gray of his muscular irises that constrict with the emphatic intensity of his gaze.

NARRATOR, METROS (V.O.)

When a prospective client is talking to you, you listen to what he is saying with his eyes. It might seem strange to say, but the luminous world is a nearly invisible world ... it is a world we do not often see. The demands of luminosity, like the demands of truth, are severe -- she has no sympathy for pretense. To find true luminosity, we must become, in a word, <u>perspicuous</u>!

UNFREEZE - LIVE ACTION CONTINUES.

ZILCH

I need for you to find something for me -- a beautiful woman, actually -- and I need you to understand that this is a very private matter.

METROS

Perhaps what you need is to hire a private detective to find this woman.

ZILCH (EYES BLAZING)

I could hire a hundred private eyes to find anything I want.
In Hollywood, we do it all the time. We hire detectives to
dig up dirt on our adversaries, and a sleazy reporter or two
later, we find ourselves in a ...
(purses lips smugly, eyes flashing)
... more favorable position of negotiation.

METROS
(trying not to yawn)
I know. I read the newspapers.

Noticeable FLAKES of ASH from a previous client's cigarette FLOAT UP
out of a brass ashtray and crawl deliberately across the shiny top of the desk
in the draft from an open window.

Zilch SWEEPS the diverting ash trail off the desk and onto the floor with
one swift movement of his empty hand.

ZILCH

Then you know I could hire a hundred private detectives
to find her -- and maybe I will. Meanwhile, I want you to
do something for me that I can't do for myself, something
that only the likes of you and your ilk can do.

METROS

Why me? There are lots of well-qualified therapists,
shrinks, and life coaches in Hollywood. There are those
who specialize in grief counseling, illness and loss, even
anger management -- which, in your case, might be
advised. You strike me as a man who knows what he wants
and has pretty much figured out how to get it. You're not
a man who needs a reality check to remind you that "she's
just not that into you."

ZILCH

Don't give me that shit! I was the sun and the stars to her,
and she means the world to me. I know it sounds corny,

but we were made for each other, and she would be the first to tell you so! But something happened that I can't explain; something just snapped. I know we had our difficulties -- we are both high-strung and demanding -- but we always reconciled, eventually, that is.

                    METROS
That is, until now.

                    ZILCH
Yeah, until now. And I just can't stand it!

                    METROS
But why me, Mr. Zilch? There must be some reason you sought me out.

                    ZILCH
Goddamn it! You wrote <u>That Book</u>, and you know it!

Zilch SLAMS his HANDS hard on the desk, stands up abruptly, and walks to the open window. Breathing deeply, shaking his head, he turns back around, accusation flaring in his eyes.

                    ZILCH (CONT'D)
You know exactly why I'm here, and it sure isn't your bedside manner -- it's that goddamned book of yours!

FREEZE-FRAME, ANGLE ON - METROS, leaning pensively on his hand, as he describes "The Book" that made him famous.

                    NARRATOR, METROS (V.O.)
Ahhhh, <u>The Book</u> ... my <u>Lost Angels Pantheon</u> -- I might have known. Gleaned from my doctoral dissertation, my internship at the Malibu Drug Rehab Center, and my shifts on the Hollywood Suicide and Crisis Hotlines, <u>The LOST ANGELS PANTHEON</u> made me a literary luminary overnight. People began to recognize themselves in the various <u>postmodern archetypes</u> I described: it was

as if I had penetrated the psychic pantheon of a litany of lost souls -- the erosion of values ... the spiritual disorientation ... the metaphysical vertigo that results in intense suffering and feelings of emptiness. It was as if I had somehow captured the personal crisis of a host of contemporary celebrities. To put it mildly, I was mobbed after I wrote The Book of the Lost Angels. Simply mobbed.

UNFREEZE - LIVE ACTION CONTINUES with Zilch pacing.

                    METROS
            (speaking dismissively)
Now, now, Mr. Zilch, perhaps it would be best if you did hire a competent private detective who could find this particular woman for you, and then he or she could initiate a constructive dialogue between the two of you.

                    ZILCH
            (confronting Metros)
That's not going to happen. I want you, the great Joe Metropolis, to help me.

                    METROS
            (parrying the thrust)
But come now, Mr. Zilch. You know that love fades, reality sets in, people change right before our eyes. I can recommend some excellent clinical psychologists who specialize in marital relations, the agonies of heartbreak, and the associated problems of self-esteem --

                    ZILCH
            (his eyes glaring like a pair of Saturday-night
            specials)
Look here, Metropolis, you're not listening to what I'm telling you. For someone who's paid to listen, you're no damn good at it! I don't want to know where she's run off to. What I really want ... what I really need to know is why!

METROS
(watching, examining)
I see … Go on, don't stop now.

ZILCH
I hate to admit it, but you're my last hope. Suddenly I feel all dead inside.

METROS
Go on.

ZILCH
I feel like I'm backed up into a dark corner, and I don't even know who or what's hitting me.

METROS
I can sympathize with your dilemma, Mr. Zilch, but before I can commit my services to this case, I want to be certain that you realize that standard psychological counseling is always available to you. I need to be sure that you are fully aware of this, for professional reasons.

ZILCH
(barely warding off defeat)
No. I won't do it. I won't submit to it, I tell you. I'm telling you now, once and for all, that I don't want any damn counseling. I want to know why! Why I feel like I'm dying all the time … why she left me in the first place … why she's not coming back … I want to know why my love was not strong enough to hold her …

(struggling between defiance and submission, he sits)
And besides breaking my heart, she stole something very valuable from me, and I want it back!

FREEZE-FRAME, ANGLE ON - ZILCH, then METROS (studying)

NARRATOR, METROS (V.O.)

So, I'm his last best hope. He's lost his gal, and he feels all dead inside. He's backed up into a dark corner, and he doesn't know who's hitting him. It's like I've heard this all before, like the voice of a hard-boiled detective in an old black-and-white movie reel. Only now, in the ultra-neo-noir of our contemporary high society, it is not the private eye who is called on to find some <u>hidden truth</u>; it is the "perspicuous eye" who is called upon to find the <u>lost beauty</u>.

UNFREEZE - LIVE ACTION CONTINUES.

METROS

What, may I ask, is this valuable thing that has, presumably, been stolen?

ZILCH

No, you may not ask. It's much too personal to discuss at this time. It's enough for me to say that something very valuable has been stolen from me, and I want it back!

METROS

I heard you the first time, Mr. Zilch. I'm simply trying to clarify the assumptions and parameters relating to issues of meaning, value, and purpose.

ZILCH

(standing again, pacing)

Cut the crap, Metropolis! You'll have plenty of time to philosophize on your own time. On my time, I want you to work <u>for me</u>, not <u>on me</u>. I want you to drop everything you're doing and start right away! I'll pay you double your going rate and all reasonable expenses ...

Zilch pauses, notices a single antiquated BOOK displayed prominently, sideways, on the otherwise sparse BOOKSHELVES.

ZILCH (CONT'D)

What the hell kind of reference library is this? It can't be your book -- it's too old. I can't even read the title.

METROS

(casually)

It's entitled The Consolation of Philosophy by Anicius Boethius. It was a bona fide best seller in medieval times.

ZILCH

(curiously, interested)

Yeah? What's it about?

METROS

It was written during the author's imprisonment, written for other prisoners on death row. Lady Philosophy -- the goddess of wisdom -- appears to the man in extremis, forsaken by fortune and suffering from tortures, as a consoling vision, of sorts, entering into conversations of high-minded ilk.

ZILCH

Sounds like the Kiss of the Spider Woman to me -- like some kind of femme fatale.

METROS

Very nearly ... but not exactly ... Now, seriously, Mr. Zilch, how can I help you?

ZILCH

(handing Metros a card)

Come to my home in Beverly Hills tonight, nine o'clock sharp, and come alone. I'll tell you everything you need to know.

As Zero Vaynilovich proceeds to depart, he turns back with a sheepish grin and inquires with uncharacteristic politeness,

ZILCH (CONT'D)

By the way, what are you going to call this case? I know guys like you always come up with a clever title.

METROS

I think I'll call this case <u>The Lost Love of the Latest Tycoon</u>. What do you think?

ZILCH

It will do just fine.

INT. METROS'S OUTER OFFICE - CONTINUOUS

As the outer office DOOR CLOSES behind Zilch, the SECRETARY, HOLLY, pretty and in her midtwenties, silhouetted, is hastily seating herself on the DESK with legs crossed, picking up a nail file, clearly ready to deny she's been eavesdropping. Metros enters, notices the ruse with disapproval.

METROS
(condescending)
Can I assume that you have already opened a case file, Holly, or were you too busy listening in?

HOLLY
(unabashed, excited)
You know, he really is a big shot, Doc. I can't wait to tell the girls down at the Alcove.

METROS

Perish the thought! You know that my client-centered approach to these philosophical investigations must be held in the strictest confidence.

HOLLY
(dejected, resumes filing)
Yeah, yeah, patient confidentiality can be such a killjoy … By the way, your wheels-of-the-week has arrived.

METROS

Really? What did he bring me this time?

Metropolis parts the curtains, PEERS out the WINDOW, notices the shadow-gray 2004 Aston Martin DB9 coupe, and SMILES.

HOLLY

I've heard of grateful patients, Doc, but this is ridiculous. He just waltzes in each week and hands over a new set of keys.

METROS

It's what we call a perk in this town, Holly. But seriously, don't you recall the severity of the mental distress and misery he carried when he was first referred to me by his employers?

HOLLY
(still filing her nails)
Yeah, yeah, he was downright suicidal.

METROS
(patiently, succinctly)
What he was, my dear, was a sensitive guy in a tough business -- neither neurotic nor crazy.

HOLLY

So you've said ...
(looking up with a hint of doubt and then conceding)
I have to admit, he was a changed man after you talked him down.
(Returns to her nails)
But I still don't get how you did it.

METROS

Simple.

(Grinning)

As always, with applied philosophy.

(Goes to the desk next to a filing cabinet and
opens a drawer, looking for something.)

NARRATOR, METROS (V.O.)

What I didn't need to tell Holly was that as a repo man
in this town, my sensitive former client had been berated
by hard-luck story after hard-luck story -- failed dot-com
executives from Silicon Valley, laid-off biotech CEOs
down in San Diego. He'd been so burdened with guilt,
remorse, and bad conscience that it had all worsened to
a level of severe depression, until it interfered with his
work. In fact, his personal sympathies had rendered him
helplessly mired in the anguish and despair of the fallen
financial highfliers -- to the point of self-loathing. His
employers and I had grave concerns.

HOLLY

(Standing and walking to Metros, takes the
blank file he's pulled from the drawer and sits
behind the desk, clearly completing the task
Metros had been starting. Looks up)

Yes, yes, philosophy. But what you never <u>did</u> explain was,
if he wasn't really sick in the first place, how did you and
your philosophy help him?

METROS

Quite simply, Holly, my philosophical counseling
began with readings and discussion of pertinent
existentialists -- Friedrich Nietzsche, who explored the
origins of bad conscience; Albert Camus, who considered
the absurdity of all modern man's dilemmas. Then I
introduced him to the Stoic philosopher Epictetus and
the concept of prohairesis, literally choice --

HOLLY
(impatiently)
Simplify, Doc. You know I don't speak Latin or Greek.

METROS
Ahem ... The breakthrough in <u>The Case of the Remorseful</u> <u>Repo Man</u> came when he grasped the true nature of reality -- that is, the dichotomy between <u>fortune</u>, or material things, and <u>judgment</u>, which is always within our power. Once he grasped these concepts and employed them in his work, he began to experience an undisturbed state of mind, which is among the tangible fruits of philosophical practice.

HOLLY
(playfully)
So <u>he</u> gets peace of mind and a newfound popularity ...
(Taps out something on the computer keyboard and turns to watch the printer emit something)

METROS
Exactly.

NARRATOR, METROS (V.O.)
What my lovely secretary is alluding to was that our repo man, once liberated from his problematic responses to all the external objects in life -- freed from the consideration that the economic recession was, in any way, up to him or within his power to abate -- found a new stoic serenity that was so contagious that the benefits of reasoning (in accordance with the <u>true nature of reality</u>) soon extended to the mournful deadbeats. And they, after talking at length with our inspired repo man, were quite relieved to have their materialistic burdens taken off their hands. He is now the most popular repo man in all of California!

HOLLY
(Takes the printed sheet, peels off the label,
and secures it to the file she took from Metros.
Looks up at him and laughs lightheartedly)
And you get a grateful patient and another set of "hot
wheels."

METROS
(grasping the keys and motioning to the door)
Specifically, a slightly used, but highly serviceable, Aston
Martin DB9 coupe, which the creditors won't miss for
a week or so and is waiting for me to drive my adoring
secretary to her luncheon engagement at the Alcove.

HOLLY
(Depositing the file in the filing cabinet, exits
through the door METROS is holding open
for her.)

EXT. BEVERLY HILTON HOTEL - EARLY EVENING

Limos and luxury cars are arriving at the circular entrance. Well-dressed
women and men, mostly women, are escorted in. ANGLE ON - LOBBY,
SIGN "Women in Film, Private Screening." We enter the International
Ballroom, arrayed in dining configuration.

ESTABLISHING SHOTS survey a scene of anxious anticipation, where well-
heeled attendees are ushered to decorous tables arrayed for optimal motion
picture viewing. FOCUS ON - one particular TABLE seems abuzz with
assiduous activity - a strikingly beautiful Asian woman (MANIFESTA) is
holding court. She is seated (unmasked) among a bevy of exotic, picturesque
women; each is wearing a feather-ornamented masquerade mask.

W.I.F. SPEAKER
(assumes the podium)
You have all heard me say that "without women there
would be no cinema." No nickelodeons. No Kiss in the
Tunnel. No Siege of Troy. No Birth of a Nation. There

15

would be nothing about Eve, no <u>Passion of Joan of Arc</u>, fewer meaningful romances, and very little drama.
(pausing for applause)
Yet in spite of our contributions to the ascent of mankind, and womankind, through the lenses of history, we remain bridled and suppressed in our efforts to move beyond the objectifying genres of women's issues and ensembles to take on subjects of serious gravity. So, tonight I am honored to introduce you all to <u>Manifesta</u>, a brilliant new champion of women's liberation, who brings a director's gravitas to the issue of violence against women.

ESTABLISHING SHOTS of the AUDIENCE clapping. ANGLE ON - the table where the beautiful MANIFESTA appears reluctant to stand and be recognized; at which point a stunning feather-masked figure, A LUMINOUS WOMAN in a shimmering-gold plunging low-cut evening gown, RISES from the seat beside Manifesta and draws her up and into a full-blown LOVER'S EMBRACE.

CLOSE ON - the WOMEN KISS deeply as the AUDIENCE APPLAUDS. PULLING AWAY - the Luminous Woman disengages and then sits, leaving Manifesta standing alone, smiling, waving …

ANGLE ON - the W.I.F. SPEAKER, who holds up a ribbon-clad SCROLL. Pulling the ribbon from the SCROLL, she unfurls the document and continues with her theatrical introduction.

W.I.F. SPEAKER (CONT'D)
While the waiters serve our dinner tonight, we are delighted to screen a sneak preview of a film that will literally take your breath away …
(waving the fancy scroll)
Each of you have been given a stylish glossy invitation -- which is not to frame and hang on the wall. It is a special invitation for you to attend the upcoming media event …
when <u>cinema takes violence to the streets</u>!

The shocking SNEAK PREVIEW begins with a PETITE BLONDE, terrified and trembling, standing shoeless and windblown atop the ARTFULLY BLOODIED "H" of the iconic HOLLYWOOD SIGN ... followed by a cinematic MONTAGE of VIOLENT ACTS: vivid, all too familiar, ultracontemporary, and recognizable CRIME SCENES -- appearing real in the reenactments.

                    Sneak Preview Narration (V.O.)
          Women of Los Angeles! You are all in danger! None of
          you are safe in this brazen city, this sepulchre by the sea!
          You cannot go to a restaurant! ... You cannot go out on a
          date! ... You cannot even go to a motion picture screening
          after-party!"

The CAMERA then TRACKS the path of a woman leaving the ballroom with the SCROOL IN HAND. CLOSE ON - the ribbon-clad SCROLL; and as it EXITS the Beverly Hilton Hotel, we exit the scene.

EXT. ZILCH'S VILLA - EVENING

We see Metros DRIVING the Aston Martin DB9 coupe up the stately, lamplit Crescent Drive, where tall palms turn to elegant fir trees. As he EXITS the DB9 coupe, the door swings gracefully upward, and he seems reluctant to let go of the handle. Finally, he WALKS up to the brightly lit ENTRANCE of the VENETIAN PALAZZO arrayed in Renaissance grandeur.

EXT/INT. ZILCH'S VENETIAN PALAZZO

We see Metropolis waiting, examining the grandiose entrance. Then, the FRONT DOOR OPENS.

                    ZILCH
          Joe Metropolis. Good. I was beginning to think I might
          have scared you off.

STANDING in the oversize ENTRANCEWAY, Zilch looks every bit the renowned writer/director/movie producer, embodying the charismatic qualities of a Hollywood motion picture tycoon in full command of his realm. He stands tall and proud, his fierce, steely eyes taking in the arrival. Then, a dark shadow of gloom appears on his face; he STEPS BACK into the FOYER.

ZILCH (CONT'D)
Come in, Metropolis. We have serious work to do.

INT. ZILCH'S INNER SANCTUM

The ROTUNDA is distinctly darker, cavernous, with low-key lighting, pools of darkness -- a chiaroscuro mise-en-scène.

ZILCH
(directing)
Take a seat over there.

ANGLE ON - a large VELVET CHAIR, then on ZILCH, who situates himself in the shadows by leaning against the ornate marble statuary of a gigantic old-world FIREPLACE, empty and dark.

METROS
Couldn't we use a little more light, Mr. Zilch? I can barely see my own hands.

ZILCH
What you can or cannot see does not concern me in the least. It is only what I can see that is of vital importance.

METROS
Okay, if you say so. But wouldn't it be helpful for both of us if we could see each other during our conversation? In my experience, direct observation can be most enlightening ...

ZILCH
Forget it, Metropolis. I don't want you to bring some blasted enlightenment into my life. I want you to help me to see more clearly in <u>the dark</u>!

18

Metropolis starts to stand up, hesitates; then, detecting a note of sincerity in the shadowy man, he decides to play along.

ZILCH (CONT'D)
Calm down, Metropolis. You're tougher than that. I know you are, or I wouldn't have hired you. And besides, it's just the way I am. It has nothing to do with you. So don't be offended. And don't expect my manners to improve. I don't have time to be circumspect, you see. My time is running out!

METROS
Okay, Mr. Zilch, it's your problem, and it's your nickel. So, how do you suggest we proceed?

ZILCH
I'll talk, you listen -- period. You can even close your eyes if you like; I won't be offended. You're just another audience out there in the dark, an audience that has become accustomed to taking in impressions solely by eye and has lost the art of listening. Believe me, I know; I'm in the business of providing the eye candy.
(beat).
But long before there were movies, there were words, ideas. Long before motion pictures, there were literal dreams of beauty. And this is what I want to tell you about.

METROS
(cozying into the velvet chair)
Please continue. I'm listening.

ZILCH
Recall the great oral traditions -- the legends, the minstrels, the poets. With words alone, they could break your heart or make a sad heart sing. With words alone, you'd know all you'd ever need to know. When we listen in the dark, the story is still out there, in the dark.

As he speaks, ZILCH begins to MOVE around the ROTUNDA, a specter of antiquity moving through SHADOWS, past STATUES, EMPTY VASES as big as the Ritz, and back to the ornamented HEARTH, the primal podium of the most ancient of orators.

> ZILCH (CONT'D)
> You see, Metropolis, the story of my life began when I met her. I was in school, immersed in my studies and fairly comfortable with my own worldview, which was moving at twenty-four frames per second. I had nearly completed my master's in film production and direction. I was sitting in on a lecture, and she was there -- as resplendent as ever -- arguing with a visiting professor about things so far over my head I couldn't follow the conversation or even imagine I ever could. <u>What star had she fallen from to land here on this planet</u>? I had to know.

Zilch comes clearly into view, and he notices Metropolis scrutinizing him. He MOVES OFF deeper into the shadows -- a disembodied VOICE now, FLOATING among the shadows in the museum-like ROTUNDA.

> ZILCH (CONT'D)
> (moving in the shadows)
> I don't know how I managed it -- I do know that I wanted it more than anything -- but somehow I joined the conversation with just enough substance and confidence for her to notice me. It didn't help that she was sleeping with the famous professor at the time ... or that I was just another celluloid protégé, strutting and fretting his hour and a half on the silver screen, another idiot full of cinematic sound and fury, signifying nothing.
>
> (pausing by a shadowy statue)
> But I tell you, when she cast her wondrous spell on me, I felt for the first time in my life that everything was possible ... that I could be more than a promising young director ... that I could achieve something lasting and artistically profound! By aspiring to her level, I could fathom the

20

mystery of creativity itself; I could harness the power of the imagination.

METROS
(interjecting with a sudden realization)
May I assume that this inspiring woman is Kaltrina Dahl? The elusive and mysterious "Blue Dahlia," whose very footsteps -- according to the local press -- are marked with epiphany?

ZILCH
(returning to the fireplace)
You may. What you clearly don't know is that everything I have accomplished, everything I am, is a result of her blessed inspiration. In her admiration, I found the sublime grandeur of literature; in her aspiration, I uncovered my authentic vision as a director; in her enthusiasm, I unearthed my passion for the stories that give life its form. Kaltrina is the essence behind all my award-winning films.

ZILCH MOVES, switches on SPOTLIGHTS lighting framed PICTURES, MOVIE POSTERS; he stops before a Greco-Roman STATUE, reaches as though to embrace the statue.

ZILCH (CONT'D)
But it wasn't simple, Metropolis; at first, she was so aloof -- completely unattainable. She was my unreachable Blue Dahlia. But reach for her, I did. And believe me, it was like reaching for the stars. Then one day, she recognized me as an embryonic artist with potential. I hadn't changed, mind you. No, she saw the possibility of something interesting in me, and out of this unformed amalgamation of sheer possibility, she created an illustrious image of me. I began to see myself in her eyes ... and I liked what I saw!

Zilch MOVES back into view, HOLDS UP his two INDEX FINGERS with his THUMBS pressed together, a director's "hand frame."

ZILCH (CONT'D)
(squinting through the handmade "frame")
For the first time, the cameras became extensions of my eyes, the frames of unexposed film, my thoughts. I could examine every scene a priori, like the facets of a diamond held within my brain and turned within my mind ... until, at last, I found that one angle, that one perfect lens, that one facet that shone with a wholly original gleam. With my darling Blue Dahlia by my side, I developed an original sense of style -- all the imagery, dialogue, music, and editing fell perfectly into place. But she was the flame within the fire; it was her intense radiance that poured through the camera's lens.

METROS
(interjecting the obvious)
She was your muse.

ZILCH
(scolds, first making his director's frame, this time framing his "audience" -- Metros; then begins moving among the statues and shadows again)
No! She was no mere muse! She was not some kind and gentle nurturer of the artistic soul. She didn't just inspire me; it was never that easy. Our bond was demanding of a perfection that is all too rare these days. But, somehow, it was attainable. Together, we excelled, and I achieved more than anyone could have achieved alone.

Zilch MOVES along the gallery of MOVIE POSTERS to another female Greco-Roman STATUE, which he addresses and EMBRACES tenderly.

ZILCH (CONT'D)
Kaltrina is certainly beautiful enough to stand in front of the cameras, but she remained out of the limelight by her own choice. Still, she was always present in the medium, like a ghost in the machine. Kaltrina is not easy

to please -- but when she is pleased ... there is nothing like it in this world!

(languishing in envelopment)

Our love was a copulation of body and soul: each kiss was a profusion of her feminine beauty, heralding the perfectibility of man. Each embrace, one long awe-inspiring, mind-expanding, breathtaking, death-defying, timber-shivering orgasm. Like art itself, she had once been unattainable ... but no longer! She was no longer the elusive unattainable Blue Dahlia; she was bloodred real, she was astonishingly hot, and she was mine!

(releasing the statue)

Did I tell you she has the body of a goddess?

METROS

(speaking matter-of-factly)

You didn't have to.

ZILCH

But that was only the beginning. The dreams that came were nothing less than Apollonian exaltations, a light-filled space in which a man can enjoy the immediate apprehension of form with godlike clarity. The applications to filmmaking were extraordinary ...

(casually viewing his posters)

Everything turned to gold. I became a high priest of Hollywood. My career blossomed, and you know the rest. We made history, and I got rich and famous. Every man wanted to be my friend; every woman wanted to have my child. I was living the high life in the radiance of her approval, the eloquence of her desire. I became a self-proclaimed motion picture artiste, a quintessential "superior man."

(turning to Metros, he forms his right hand
into a fist)

Like the diamond I'd learned to hold and turn in my mind, I became hard. So bright, I made cinematic history with every movie reel. So hard, I became a Hollywood hyperborean.

METROS
(curious, studious)
A hyperborean?

ZILCH
(matter-of-factly)
You know, a race of mythical creatures who live beyond the north wind.

METROS
I see.

ZILCH
I began to enjoy the supreme confidence of my own genius. Then one day, those beautiful eyes blinked; her lovely voice faltered. It was almost imperceptible at first, but she drifted away ... out of reach ... out of sight ... and then she was gone!

Zilch MOVES about the ROTUNDA with its gallery of MOVIE POSTERS and larger-than-life-size STATUES one more time as he turns off the SPOTLIGHTS, slowly, theatrically, one by one.

ZILCH (CONT'D)
I tried to focus on my work, my art, to prove to myself I could do it alone. The more I tried, the less it mattered. Sure, sure, the wheels of Tinseltown still turned for me, doors were opened, actors and actresses swooned; but I knew I'd lost my edge. The more I tried to recapture the creative spark, the more stylistic, the more derivative my films became, the more extravagant, the more degenerate, the more lewd, the more violent. The further I fell from artistic grace, the more I had to rely on spectacle and the more grotesque it all became ... until, at last -- damn it all -- my movies have become nothing but a museum ... a museum unto myself!

24

Zilch POURS HIMSELF into a large VELVET CHAIR and covers his face with his hands: a muffled sobbing of unbearable sadness.

> METROS
> (thoughtfully, counseling)
> I think I follow you, Mr. Zilch, and perhaps I can help you in some way. As I recall, you did mention Apollo, the luminous god of the "plastic arts." Speaking in the insightful terms of Arthur Schopenhauer, the definitive criterion of a philosopher's ability is the gift of regarding man's perceptions as mere phantoms and dream pictures.

METROS STANDS and WALKS over to a nearby STATUE.

> METROS (CONT'D)
> (eyeing the statue)
> The only problem I have with your story is the modern existentialist's assumption that any experience that is intelligible is already an illusion -- that our perceptions are, necessarily, creative, illusory, and, therefore, contrived.

> ZILCH
> (angrily, looking up)
> Are you calling me a liar, Metropolis? Because if you are --

> METROS
> No, not a liar in the pejorative sense, but an artistic creator by nature.

> ZILCH
> (leaning forward in the plush velvet chair)
> Then say what you mean, dammit! This is hard enough for me as it is.

> METROS
> What I mean to say is that our private worlds are perceived somewhat creatively. They stream through the faculty of the imagination like a fiery liquid. Only by conveniently forgetting

25

some things and creating others can we live with any sense of security and consistency. After all, we are constantly creating subjects ... creating, perhaps, even <u>lost objects</u>.

ZILCH
(with disappointment)
It still sounds like you don't believe me.

METROS
On the contrary, I am listening very carefully, like you asked me to do, and I am simply considering the possibility that there might be more than one side to this story.

ZILCH
I try to tell you my story, from my own point of view, and you criticize me. If this is philosophy, keep it! To tell you the truth, I have absolutely no faith in philosophy whatsoever ...

Zilch RISES to his feet and gazes anxiously about the room, as if looking for an Exit sign; then he TURNS BACK abruptly.

ZILCH (CONT'D)
But <u>she does</u>! Kaltrina read <u>your book,</u> and she told me how much she admired your damned insights. That's why I'm standing here in the dark, allowing you to criticize me in my own house, under my own roof!

METROS
Calm down, Mr. Zilch. You're tougher than that. I know you are, or I would never have critiqued your story. And besides, it's just the way of the world. It has nothing to do with you.

ZILCH
All right, all right, Metropolis, you win. I'll try not to be offended. And I don't need an echo in my own palazzo to tell me that my time is running out!

METROS

Fair enough; I won't repeat the obvious. But I am curious as to the nature of the <u>stolen object</u> you mentioned previously. It could help me with my inquiries on your behalf.

ZILCH

(abruptly, pacing)

Forget it, Metropolis. I've told you too much already. You just find out <u>why</u> my beautiful Blue Dahlia left me -- the real reason -- and leave the rest to me.

Taking this as a cue to leave, Metropolis walks away from the statue and presses the issue.

METROS

Is it safe to assume, then, that you know exactly where she is?

ZILCH

(stops pacing)

Not quite. It's much too painful for me to endure all the emasculating details, but I do have people in my employ that can provide you with that kind of information on a need-to-know basis.

METROS

Then how do you suggest I proceed?

ZILCH

(casually, then challenging)

You start by having lunch tomorrow at the Café Med on Sunset ... Meanwhile, you might want to consult with that bodacious philosopher friend of yours!

METROS

You mean Anicius Boethius and his <u>Consolation of Philosophy</u>?

ZILCH
(sarcastically, painfully)
Yeah. Ask him how much <u>consolation</u> there is when you
know deep down that she's doing her nightly visitations in
<u>someone else's prison cell!</u>

EXT. CAFE MEDITERRANEAN - DAY

Metros SITS at a curbside TABLE at an awning-covered patio, on the
SUNSET STRIP, with a prominent view of the street scene, an espresso cup
in front of him. A MAN with a dark suit and sunglasses enters (looks like
a PI); Metros leans forward attempting to draw his attention, but the man
does not acknowledge him. A COUPLE, obviously tourists, give Metros a
second look, as if ascertaining his importance; they look disappointed. The
WAITER APPROACHES.

WAITER
(plainly impatient)
Are you ready to order, sir?

METROS
No, thank you. Not just yet.

The waiter steps away, irritated. Metros sips his espresso, looks at his watch.
He looks stumped -- could this be a waste of time? He downs the last dregs
and reaches for his wallet.

Then a young LATINO MAN wearing a Dodgers' jersey and mirrored
aviator sunglasses crosses the street, APPROACHES, STOPS on the
sidewalk on the other side of the barrier in front of Metros.

LATINO MAN
(telling, not asking)
Hey, Señor, you want to buy a star map.

METROS
(enigmatically, gazing into the mirrored
sunglasses)
Thank you, but I'm not quite sure …

LATINO MAN
I am sure, Señor. You want to buy this star map.

METROS
(finally, perceptively)
Okay, I get it …

Metros pulls out a twenty-dollar bill and hands it to the young man. The man stands there waiting, disapprovingly. Metros hands him another twenty-dollar bill, and the man walks away, saying nada.

Metros examines the STAR MAP: "Stars' Homes, plus Sightseeing, Walk of Fame, Entertainment, and Discount Coupons," along with the assurance "Revised Every 90 Days." He opens it and notices a hand-drawn CIRCLE around a portion of Mulholland Drive, along with the name BYRON HARMSWAY, a well-known writer, and a PHONE NUMBER, which Metros DIALS on his cell phone.

ANSWERING MACHINE
(a sultry female voice)
Hello. If you've dialed this number, you already know with whom you'd like to speak. However, we are exercising our right to privacy at this time. Please hang up, or leave a message and then wait patiently until we decide whether or not to call you back.

METROS
(unfazed, with sardonic civility)
Hello. My name is Joe Metropolis, and I would like to speak with Byron Harmsway about Kaltrina Dahl. In the event this conversation is deemed suitable, you may reach me anon by return call.

Metros exits the sidewalk café, and as he approaches his reappropriated DB9, a RINGTONE.

                    METROS (CONT'D)
          Hello. Metropolis here …

Metros HEARS a soft-spoken, male VOICE with perfect diction, a noticeable lilt, like a summer breeze through wind chimes.

                    LEOPOLD
          I am Mr. Harmsway's personal assistant. Can you come
          right away?

EXT. MULHOLLAND DRIVE - DAY

The DB9 SPEEDS along MULHOLLAND DRIVE, coming to an abrupt stop at a closed GATE protecting an overly large Southern California manse.

EXT. HARMSWAY'S CHATEAU/FRONT GATE - DAY

Metros stares at the gate from inside the car. He looks around; but before he finds a buzzer, the gate starts to open slowly. A SECURITY GUARD appears, says nothing, signals Metros.

Metros looks pained as he drives the DB9 at a snail's pace behind the security guard, who walks slowly in front of the car.

Metros STANDS in front of a huge WOODEN DOOR, rings the doorbell -- BELLS TOLL. The door opens slowly; LEOPOLD appears -- a petite, rather delicate man wearing a lavender satin shirt.

                    LEOPOLD
          (ushering Metros in)
          Dr. Metropolis, I presume. I'm so glad that you're here.

INT. HARMSWAY'S CHATEAU - DAY

Metros ENTERS a type of minstrel's gallery in the hillside chateau, overlooking a great room: opulent, high ceilings.

                    LEOPOLD
        He's cleaning his gun again, and I'm afraid that something
        terrible is going to happen.

                    METROS
        Are you sure he's up for a visitor?

Leopold GLIDES almost on tiptoes, LEADS Metros into the clean, well-lighted space, with filtered sunlight, sparse furnishings. Jasmine and honeysuckle can be seen through the sunroom windows at the far end of the CONSERVATORY.

                    LEOPOLD
            (sheepishly)
        To be honest, Dr. Metropolis, I didn't tell him you were
        coming.

Metros, surprised, GLARES at the diminutive man.

                    LEOPOLD (CONT'D)
            (whispering, but emphatic)
        I'm hoping that you can help him.

Leopold KNOCKS, half-opens the DOOR of a handsome LIBRARY, with a crystal chandelier, floor-to-ceiling BOOKSHELVES, an expansive BOW WINDOW overlooking the manicured gardens, and a built-in BAR that is stocked as fully as the bookshelves. Leopold opens the door wide, enters; Metros follows.

                    LEOPOLD (CONT'D)
        Dr. Metropolis is here to see you, Byron. Please be so kind
        as to give him your full attention.

BYRON HARMSWAY does not get up to greet Metros or even look up. Aged and withered, the once well-muscled masculine frame is not so now -- it is bent over a large mahogany partner's DESK, a wisp of gray-brown hair falling over his sharply defined brow. Before him, the minimalist mechanical parts of an ANTIQUE REVOLVER, which he is busy assembling -- thereby placing SIX BULLETS, one by one, into the empty chambers.

> BYRON HARMSWAY
> Well, that's enough of that!

Byron flips the loading gate closed, thumbs the hammer to "half-cock," spins the cylinder, and lowers the barrel to a firing position, AIMING directly at Metros's chest.

> BYRON HARMSWAY (CONT'D)
> (addressing Metros)
> If I've learned anything about human nature, it is this: when you need a weapon, you usually need it badly -- you should always keep it well oiled and fully loaded ... You see, a handgun, like the mind of a human being, abhors a vacuum.

> METROS
> It's not what goes into the empty chambers of the human psyche that concerns me, Mr. Harmsway; it's <u>what</u> and, more importantly, <u>when</u> and <u>where</u> that hidden drama decides to burst out.

> BYRON HARMSWAY
> (waving the firearm casually)
> Finally, a philosopher with balls!

Byron points the revolver upward, drawing the cylinder close to his ear, as if he were listening to the assuring mechanics that move the atoms and the stars, as he uncocks the hammer.

> BYRON HARMSWAY (CONT'D)
> (placing weapon on desk)
> She sent you to help me, didn't she?

METROS

If you mean Kaltrina Dahl, then no. I've never met her.

BYRON HARMSWAY

Well, who sent you then? Who the hell sent Joe freakin'
Metropolis to help little old me?

METROS

I'm not at liberty to divulge that information, Mr.
Harmsway.

BYRON HARMSWAY

Why the hell not?

METROS

It's a matter of professional ethics. As you should know,
confidentiality is of paramount importance to both a
philosophical counselor and his client, as we endeavor to
explore the darkest recesses of the human mind.

BYRON HARMSWAY

I hear the words ...

Byron Harmsway PAUSES momentarily, STARING down at the loaded
revolver as if he is struggling to resist the urge to perform another
mechanical maintenance operation, then and there.

BYRON HARMSWAY (CONT'D)
(looking up, brightening)

I can appreciate your position, Joe. As a journalist and a
war correspondent, I used the same words to cover my
ass ... Nevertheless, it doesn't seem right that you should
miraculously appear out of nowhere at a time like this. It
doesn't seem right that someone is in charge and I can't
know who it is. That just doesn't seem fair, does it?

METROS

Is that a philosophical question, Mr. Harmsway?

                    BYRON HARMSWAY
          Indeed it is. Indeed it is.

Byron sends Leopold away callously with a wave of his hand.

                    BYRON HARMSWAY (CONT'D)
          Sit down, Joe. And call me Byron, for Pete's sake -- we're
          both on the same side of the typewriter.

Metros SITS in a CHAIR in front of the desk while Byron WALKS, rather
stiffly, over to the bar. He POURS WHISKEY from a monogrammed
DECANTER into two good-size CRYSTAL GLASSES.

                    BYRON HARMSWAY (CONT'D)
                 (offering up a glass)
          Drink?

                    METROS
          No, thank you. I'm my own designated driver today. I
          drove here to find out something about Kaltrina Dahl, and
          I have reason to believe you can help me.

Byron shrugs, knocks back one of the drinks in one gulp, then he carries
the full glass to the desk and retakes his seat.

                    BYRON HARMSWAY
          You think that I can help you with Kaltrina? You've got
          to be kidding.

                    METROS
          Well, I have to admit, my instructions do appear to be
          rather vague.

                    BYRON HARMSWAY
          That woman damn near ruined my life. <u>To have something</u>
          so marvelously erotic and romantic, and then <u>not to have</u>
          <u>it</u>! She wounded me, Joe, in parts unknown.

METROS
(pressing, studying Byron)
Wounded you in parts unknown to whom?

BYRON HARMSWAY
I felt like my soul, or something, came right out of my
body -- like you'd pull a silk handkerchief out of a pocket --
and it flew all around; and when it came back again, it
wasn't quite dead, but it wasn't folded the way it was before.
And that wasn't all she took from me.

METROS
Go on. You're saying that Kaltrina actually took something
from you?

BYRON HARMSWAY
Yes, dammit, she took something from me ... and she left
me a <u>depleted pocket</u>!

METROS
I get the metaphor, Byron, but you are a world-famous writer
whose novels have invigorated movies. You've created a
great larger-than-life persona; you've accomplished more
in your lifetime than most can even dream of. You have
everything a man could want --

BYRON HARMSWAY
Yeah, yeah, I was living life in the sweet good and plenty
of the American dream. Everything was roses, cigars,
champagne, and chocolates -- that is, until I met her ...
And then, <u>wham bam</u>! This self-proclaimed realist, who
writes about dramatic action and bloodshed, finds out
for himself what the action and bloodshed is all about.
She wounded me, I tell you! And some wounds leave you
empty ... they just don't heal!

METROS
(inquisitively)
It sounds to me like Kaltrina Dahl, who was obviously with you for some time, is no longer with you now. <u>Do you happen to know why</u>?

BYRON HARMSWAY
(agitated, empties his drink)
No. But I wish I did. If you ask me, it was all a dirty trick. One day she's with you with her lofty ideals -- as a writer, your vision expands; as a lover, you revel in the exaltation ... And then, just when a man is content with the appurtenances of his own success, just when he is beginning to bask in the glow of his own advent as an artiste ... she leaves you flat. It's killing me, Joe.
(fingering a single bullet)
Not knowing the meaning of life is hard enough for a man like me, but it can be tolerated. What I can't tolerate is not knowing what I did wrong! Now that she has waltzed so damn exquisitely, so profoundly into my life, I feel lost without her intimacy. <u>The unbearable sadness</u> that she left me with is even worse than the <u>meaninglessness</u> I had to endure before she came into my life!

METROS
So, if I understand you correctly, your unrequited love of this woman is even more unbearable than the most pressing of philosophical questions?

BYRON HARMSWAY
(defiant, glaring)
Don't you try to trap me, Joe. Don't you even try. I'll blow your head off!

BYRON PICKS UP the handgun, and after waving it threateningly at Metros, he TAKES AIM and FIRES into the BOOKSHELVES. He FIRES again as Metros FALLS BACKWARD in the CHAIR. Dusting himself off,

Metros examines a slew of previous BULLET HOLES in the shelved books, replaces the overturned chair, and stands calmly behind it.

> METROS
> (sarcastically)
> Trying to rewrite history, are we, Byron?

> BYRON HARMSWAY
> (putting the gun down)
> No, Dr. Philosopher. You didn't look carefully enough. I aimed well, and I only targeted <u>Contemporary Literature</u>.
> (beat)
> You see, I consider each one of those blasted authors to be my rival. Frankly, this whole business of love and sex and artistic inspiration is nothing but a dirty trick!

> METROS
> (moves from behind the chair)
> You don't really believe that life and love are nothing but a dirty trick?

BYRON empties his glass, pauses momentarily to study the beveled crystal facets, and then he begins to explain.

> BYRON HARMSWAY
> One day you get it and you think you're happy, but you know something's missing ... and she shows you what's missing and you want to believe her, but you can't believe her because she is unreliable -- and next thing you know, you wake up and find you're alone again. It's nothing but a low-down dirty rotten trick!

> METROS
> (sits down casually on the desk)
> Come now, Byron, is it really as bad as all that? You know, when <u>Eros</u> and <u>Philos</u> -- that is, erotic love and intellectual attraction -- fail to satisfy our emotional needs, the Greeks

suggested that we consider a third and higher form of affection: that is, <u>Agape</u>, which seeks nothing in return.

> BYRON HARMSWAY
> (agitated, becoming unstable)
> Oh, balls! You give me concepts while I sing for my supper! Concepts are no good at all for a man in my condition. Hell, I pride myself in being a man of action, <u>a man of decisive action</u>! I live by a code I can live with!
> (picks up and fondles the gun)
> I keep my weapon handy, clean, and well oiled, and I strive to keep my mind in a clean, well-lighted place. For me, the shortest answer to any question that disturbs me is just to do the thing! Concepts are no good at all for a man in my position!

METROS STANDS UP abruptly and EXITS the library to avoid becoming an inadvertent target for Byron's increasing angst.

> BYRON HARMSWAY (CONT'D)
> (shouting after Metros)
> In the beginning there was darkness, and then there were concepts, but still there was nothing! It's still nothing, Metropolis! Nothing at all to me …

INT/INT. HARMSWAY'S CHATEAU - CONTINUOUS

Leopold confronts Metros as Metros DARTS OUT of the LIBRARY. We follow the conversation across the CHATEAU INTERIOR.

> LEOPOLD
> (desperate)
> Do you think you can help him, Dr. Metropolis?

> METROS
> I'm afraid not. Many literary accounts describe this condition of personal "dis-ease" and despair as a sort of <u>existential vacuum</u>. But Byron Harmsway did not come to

me at an agreeably conversant, philosophically assessable stage of his disease.

                         LEOPOLD
Isn't there anything you can do?

                         METROS
I really don't think so. From my point of view, he is too afraid -- armed with a loaded gun, a bottle of whiskey, and an empty pocket. He appears to be so afraid of the nothingness that he can't stop hunting it.

                         LEOPOLD
Isn't that somewhat ambiguous, Doctor?

                         METROS
Yeah, you're right about that. And it's too bad … because moral ambiguity is my business.

EXT/INT. MULHOLLAND DRIVE (SCENIC OVERLOOK) - SUNSET

Metros, the Aston Martin DB9 parked at a panoramic LA OVERLOOK, PHONES Zilch, who answers from a FILM EDITING SUITE. The conversation INTERCUTS.

                         ZILCH
            (impatient)
So, what do you have for me, Metropolis?

                         METROS
Unfortunately, not very much. I learned nothing new about Ms. Dahl, other than she might have also taken something valuable from Byron Harmsway. Sadly, the poor fellow displays symptoms of a malaise similar to yours, only worse.

                         ZILCH
Really? Now I almost feel sorry for the bastard. You know that writers can be insufferably sensitive. Maybe I'll throw

the poor sap a bone. Perhaps I'll offer to make a movie out of the worst thing he's ever written ...

METROS
(curious and intrigued)
And what, may I ask, is the worst thing that Byron Harmsway has ever written?

ZILCH
(casually yet emphatic)
It's <u>Much Ado About Nada</u>, of course.

We see HOLLYWOOD DARKENING via TIME LAPSE - from Hollywood Hills to the LA skyline - CITY LIGHTS blinking, sparkling, then DISSOLVING to a scene of BURNING BUILDINGS, CLOSE ON - a torrent of FLAMES (foreshadowing the latest STUDIO/BACKLOT FIRE).

EXT. COSMOPOLITAN STUDIOS/BACKLOT (FIRE AFTERMATH) - DAY

Metros and Zilch STROLL through the CHARRED REMAINS of the STUDIO BACKLOT: the faux streets and neighborhoods are still smoldering in the afternoon sun. Metros notices strewn pieces of metal and wire from the EMPIRE STATE BUILDING replica and the BROOKLYN BRIDGE; he notices the damp and matted fur of the once animatronic KING KONG EXHIBIT. They MOVE through the burned-out ruins of a massive VIDEO and FILM LIBRARY, and we are struck by thousands of FILM REELS and melted VIDEOCASSETTES sprawled in a heap with fallen I-beams and girders; diminishing plumes of black smoke are wafting -- the last remains of a vast collection of analog videotape.

METROS
(suspiciously)
You didn't have anything to do with this conflagration, did you?

Zilch KICKS ASIDE a pile of JAGGED GLASS, as though he were swatting a flea.

ZILCH

Certainly not!

(gives Metros a steely look)

I wouldn't have to. All I would have to do is suggest that it might not be a bad idea, and somehow something like this would manage to happen -- if not immediately, then within a season. Things like this, like the wildfires of Los Angeles, are perennial occurrences.

METROS

(studying Zilch)

Somehow I don't find your statement all that comforting.

(beat)

And what about Byron Harmsway?

ZILCH

(coolly, now surveying the fire's remains)

What about him?

(not looking at Metros)

NARRATOR, METROS (V.O.)

I'd learned first thing that morning that Byron Harmsway's body had been found on the floor of one of the studio's burned-out soundstages with three bullets in his chest. And it didn't escape me that my client, the very man before me surveying the fire's damage almost as if watching a particularly well-composed montage, may have considered the late writer a rival. Still, Zilch didn't seem to be hiding anything, and he didn't strike me as a murderer.

ZILCH

(turning to Metros)

The police already said it was an open-and-shut case, you know -- arson/suicide.

METROS

No wonder murder mysteries are a thing of the past in this town.

Zilch gives Metros a dismissive look, and then he turns his gaze outward, over the vastness of the smoldering ruins.

> ZILCH
>
> It's not just murder mysteries, but great dramas, great directors, great artistic visions -- the golden age, the star machine ... I can remember a time when Hollywood Studios had more stars under contract than there are in heaven. Then it all just died!

> METROS
>
> I believe it's what we call <u>stasis</u>, in modern rhetorical terms.

> ZILCH
>
> What's that supposed to mean? I thought we were talking about <u>my world</u>.

> METROS
> (patiently explaining)
>
> "<u>Stasis in the arts is tantamount to death</u>" -- it is an axiom that relates to both language and culture. I believe that this <u>stasis in the arts</u> might somehow relate to your world as well.

> ZILCH
> (another dismissive look)
>
> Maybe you should keep your axioms to yourself ... We're in Hollywoodland!

Zilch and Metros STEP OVER a makeshift POLICE BARRIER into the ruins of the KING KONG attraction. They step past the beast's right fist, closer to the center of the tram bridge, and look up into its face. Still clinging to the cables above the collapsing bridge, Kong's defiant torso, with its fabulous woolly exterior, has been reduced to a carcass of smoldering fur. Metros LEANS CLOSE TO the charred remains of the creature; he strokes a clump of matted fur.

NARRATOR, METROS (V.O.)

I can't help myself. Visions of the former glory of this now smoldering, impotent frame flood through me. And I can almost feel the sheer terror and glee as the thirty-foot, seven-ton animatronic beast pounds his massive fists, shaking the very bridge I now stand on. I can almost hear the shrieks of the tram's wide-eyed occupants; feel their utter awe and admiration. It's hard to believe this beast will never roar, never move again.

METROS
(still looking at the ruined Kong)

It's a shame that this attraction was totally destroyed by the fire. It was like a shrine for so many people.

(turning his gaze to Zilch, probing, with irony)

It's almost as if we set him up and then we killed him.

(beat)

His only fault was his being too big -- he had too much "heart" for our liking.

ZILCH
(audacious)

Don't worry about it, Metropolis. We'll build it up even better than before. Studio sets, as you know, are eternally recurrent! In his place, we'll erect the image of a new Superman, followed by a litany of superheroes, all with supernatural powers!

METROS
(takes a step away from Kong and turns to
face Zilch; disapproving)

But isn't that a bit dubious, Mr. Zilch, considering your previously artful and highly cultured films? Isn't it a bit onerous to suggest that mankind's virtues and strengths are derived from supernatural sources?

ZILCH
(waxing grandiose)
Not just supernatural, my dear philosopher, but extra-
terrestrial!

Zilch SPREADS HIS ARMS wide before him as though he were personally
opening the curtains of a Saturday matinee.

ZILCH (CONT'D)
Imagine that the source of all power and glory, all strength
and resolve, would be visited upon our children's children
by a fleet of superheroes that has nothing to do with our
ways of thinking or history, our cultures, or even our
innate intelligence -- having instead been conveniently
delivered from afar, like a pepperoni pizza!

METROS
(obviously dismayed)
Actually, I can't imagine it. To me, that would be a great
tragedy.

ZILCH
Oh, that's not the worst of it. It's not just a new superhero
bonanza we have here -- it doesn't stop there. The
suspension of disbelief might even extend to the point
where all psychological and sociological ills that afflict
mankind are literally zapped here from outer space!

METROS
And you would endorse such foolish thinking for the sake
of entertainment?

ZILCH
I don't endorse anything, Metropolis; I just project the
pictures on the wall. Without my beautiful Blue Dahlia
to inspire me to greater artistic heights, there is always
superstition to portray -- blatantly, extravagantly, and with
visual special effects.

The charred cables creak, and the massive animatronic beast shudders, as if it might finally crash completely to the ground. ZILCH and METROS hurry along. But Metros turns back for one final look.

                    METROS
Really, Mr. Zilch, doesn't such aggrandizement of superstition, as you call it, tend to create an atmosphere that erodes all our human responsibilities?

                    ZILCH
          (following METROS's gaze)
Come now, Metropolis, don't be so serious. It's not as if the bastions of Western civilization were reduced to rubble by the hawking of medieval sorcery to unwitting schoolchildren. It's not as if Hollywood studios were employing mass-marketing strategies to promote and exploit the black cauldrons of witchcraft. You don't think something like that could happen in this day and age, do you?

                    METROS
          (resigned, yet defiant)
Perhaps not. But I do advocate a certain level of social responsibility in my philosophical practice, and it seems to me that such responsibility would limit the promotion of ideologies that encourage mass stupidity.

                    ZILCH
          (emphatically)
Oh, you can't blame me for that, Metropolis. Mass stupidity was here long before I came to this town.

EXT. SUNSET BOULEVARD/PRODUCTION CREW - DAY

ESTABLISHING SHOTS - Extreme long shots of the STREETSCAPE. ZOOM TO - a TALL BUILDING with a large painted BILLBOARD, being PAINTED OVER with silver/white reflective aluminum PAINT.

CLOSE ON - a FILMMAKING CREW, PRODUCTION TRUCKS line the foreground. Multiple MOVIE PROJECTORS, LASERS, LIGHTS, and SPEAKERS are being arranged in the ALLEYS of adjacent BUILDINGS. A DIRECTORIAL WOMAN (MANIFESTA) -- the Queen Bee -- appears to be directing the dutiful swarm of engineers.

CLOSER ON - MANIFESTA is joined by a MYSTERIOUS WOMAN wearing a feathered MASK and a magnificent peacock feather printed silk dress. The women walk slowly, gracefully, arm in arm along the hallowed boulevard, while the PRODUCTION CREW "appears" to SHIFT INTO FAST MOTION (with the artistry of TIME LAPSE cinematography).

EXT/INT. LA STREETS/METROS'S UBER CAR - A FEW DAYS LATER

Metros DRIVES nimbly along the Pacific Coast Highway, Malibu Hills/ Palisades, <u>down</u> Santa Monica Blvd. to HOLLYWOOD FOREVER MEMORIAL PARK. EXT.: A nearly new basalt-black PORSCHE CARRERA GT. INT: Metros wears a black suit and tie, black sunglasses; windblown hair. He spots the "INFINITY SIGN," TURNS into the ENTRANCE, stops at the GATE HOUSE, reluctantly hands the keys to a VALET GUY.

EXT. HOLLYWOOD FOREVER GRAVEYARD - DAY (CONTINUOUS)

ESTABLISHING SHOT - the HOLLYWOOD SIGN, framed by palm trees. Entering the Memorial Park, Metros FOLLOWS an USHER LADY to the VIP section of the star-studded CEMETERY, passing rows of carved HEADSTONES, newer versions with life-size laser-etched FACES turned eerily sideways, looking on. ZILCH is STANDING with a small BEVY of invited MOURNERS dressed in black with fashionable veils; he is munching a chocolate chip cookie. Metros spots a coffee dispenser among the linen-covered tables and folding chairs; he pumps away, to clear his head.

ZILCH
(a mouthful of chocolate chips)
Well, well, the sage of the fallen angels! Now that you're here, we can get this digital interment over with.

46

Faced by a curious gaggle of Hollywood's finest, Metros is at a loss for words. Not so, Zilch, the quintessential showman, STEPS UP to the OPEN COFFIN and the telltale RECTANGULAR PIT.

ZILCH (CONT'D)
Ladies and gentleman, as Eric von Stroheim once said, in his eulogy for D. W. Griffith, "In Hollywood, you're only as good as your last picture," and I believe that to be true for a writer as well. So, today it is my great pleasure to announce that I will be directing the movie adaptation of Byron Harmsway's last novel -- as well as his digital video Life Story, which we will begin filming today.

Zilch RAISES HIS HANDS to the sky as if he were repositioning the planets. In no time at all, MOVIEMAKING EQUIPMENT begins to roll out of several nondescript PRODUCTION TRUCKS onto the cemetery lawn: dollies, tracks, booms, lights, reflectors, and steady-cams appear with their operators; like a school of fish that moves en masse. The production staff, set design, talent, grips, lighting, rigging, and sound mixers dash on.

LOOKING ON from the filmmaking hustle and bustle in the foreground to the HOLLYWOOD SIGN looming in the distance -- as bold as any cinema production de rigueur -- Metros only shrugs.

Then Metros TURNS BACK and is surprised by an unscripted scene: ANGLE ON - ZILCH, leaning into the OPEN COFFIN, searching for something beneath THE CADAVER, and then RIFFLING through the dead man's pockets. Metros APPROACHES Zilch; they are out of earshot of the others standing nearby.

METROS
(in a hushed but accusatory tone)
So, you actually did see Byron Harmsway the evening before he died?

ZILCH
(quips)
I told you that I might, and I didn't say that I hadn't.

METROS

You also told me that you had nothing to do with this deadly business. Are you sure that the dearly departed Byron Harmsway didn't <u>offend you</u> in some way?

ZILCH

(ushering Metros silently into the Griffith Lawn, a more secluded part of the VIP cemetery at the moment)

Look, Metropolis, I'd snuff out the sun if it offended me -- or I'd have Special Effects do it for me ... The idea of Harmsway galls me. Yes, he bothered me. But he is only a mask -- it is the emptiness behind the mask that I chiefly hate. It is the emptiness behind the mask that I intended to eliminate.

METROS

You're speaking cinematically, I suppose? You don't really mean what you're saying literally, do you?

ZILCH

(turning and strolling toward the Garden of Legends, nonchalantly)

In Hollywood, we take our allusions seriously.

METROS

(following Zilch, waxing indignant)

In that case, let me ask you directly: Did you or did you not have anything to do with Byron Harmsway's death, be it murder or suicide?

ZILCH

No and yes. No, I did not murder him, and yes, I suppose I had something to do with his suicide ... You see, when I agreed to produce his last novel -- as I said, to throw him a bone -- he and I both knew that it was a piece of garbage, and we both knew that neither of us would ever produce anything but garbage ever again. What's worse, <u>we both suspected we knew why</u>.

                    METROS

Can you tell me?

                    ZILCH

All I did was tighten the screw by helping him to feel like he was finally <u>finished</u>!

                    METROS

That's either the kindest or the cruelest thing I have ever heard!

                    ZILCH

          (sarcastically)
You might say that Kaltrina and I both <u>finished him off</u>! Like a one-two punch!

                    METROS

          (incredulous)
But you don't really believe that, Mr. Zilch, do you? You can't actually believe that!

                    ZILCH

I'm telling you about a situation, as it exists, as it was created. Neither you nor I have to believe it. In other words, Mr. Philosopher, welcome to my world.

WALKING through the Garden of Legends, they move past the swan-filled LAKE surrounding a white marble MAUSOLEUM, where they approach an elegant GRAVE MARKER for Tyrone Power: a MARBLE BENCH flanked on one end with an upright BOOK with masks of Comedy and Tragedy; the horizontal BENCH is engraved with the words "<u>Good Night, Sweet Prince</u> …" (*Hamlet*).

METROS

(dejected)

Your world seems to be perfectly suited for the self-defeating, Mr. Zilch. Perhaps you and I are also finished.

ZILCH

(directing Metros to the marble bench)

Snap out of it, Metropolis. I'm going to make it up to poor, suicidal Byron Harmsway. I'm going to give him a far better afterlife than he ever had in reality. It will be eternal; it will be recurrent, and there will be residuals! Besides, I need you now more than ever. I just got a hot new lead -- do you want me to show it to you or not?

METROS

(reading the Tyrone Power-bench engravings)

What's this? "The Fall of a Sparrow ... Good Night, Sweet Prince ... Flights of Angels Sing Thee to Thy Rest" ...?

ZILCH

(impatiently, he sits)

It's from Shakespeare's Hamlet!

(patting the bench)

Take a seat, Metropolis ... Tyrone Power won't mind; his sun has already set.

Metros hesitates, then he joins Zilch on the BENCH. Zilch REACHES into his jacket pocket and pulls out THE SCROLL, slowly unfurling it for Metros to see the PHOTOGRAPHS embedded within the scroll's textual content. ANGLE ON - METROS, visibly SHOCKED by something he sees in the photographs.

METROS

She looks so familiar. This woman looks very much like that actress who was shot in the face by that crazed music producer. What was her name?

ZILCH

Her name was Darla Darkcity, and she was <u>allegedly</u> shot in the face.

METROS

Not to split hairs, Mr. Zilch, but Darla Darkcity was <u>definitely</u> shot in the face. I remember those morbid crime-scene photographs all too well. The only thing that was <u>alleged</u> about the sordid affair was <u>who it was that pulled the trigger</u>. It wasn't clear whether it was him or her.

ZILCH

(brandishing the scroll)

Right you are. And now that your memory is working, take a good look at this head shot, and don't even think about pardoning the pun.

METROS

(studying the head shot)

It really looks like Darla Darkcity, but it doesn't look exactly like her. As I recall, Darla was somewhat older when she died … it's a truly beautiful photograph, that's for sure. This is either an earlier head sh-- I mean, <u>portrait</u> of Darla, or it might be her twin sister … But how can that be?

ZILCH

(with unmistakable chagrin)

You know it's not actually a head shot, don't you?

(points to the photograph)

Look closely, Mr. Philosopher. It's a positive print from a director's dailies.

METROS

(gasps; studies the photo)

That can't be right.

NARRATOR, METROS (V.O.)

Not quite having gotten over the shock of seeing this reconstruction of a beauty so thoroughly shattered, I'm now having a hard time believing the image -- which looks as exquisite, as professional as any top-flight museum-quality photography to me -- could truly have been taken from the daily rushes of a motion picture. Still, my client, who is in the position to know, is sitting next to me, with an assured, bemused grin.

METROS

I don't understand ...

ZILCH

Neither do I, Metropolis. Neither do I. But if I'm not mistaken -- and in matters of technical cinematography, I rarely am -- there is one hell of a <u>new director in this town</u>!

METROS

(fondling the scroll)
How does this photograph, this outtake, tie in with Kaltrina Dahl?

ZILCH

(a look of abject sadness)
Here's one thing I know for sure: Find this new director in town, and you'll find Kaltrina Dahl.

METROS

(dismissive)
I wouldn't know where to look.

ZILCH

I've gotta get back to filming the treatment of Byron's digital life story -- for the DVDs and his rented plot in cyberspace. But meanwhile, the physical "source" of this dark tragedy is still right here with us. Darla's still here.

METROS
(looking around the graveyard)
You mean to say that Darla Darkcity is still here … in
Hollywood Forever?

Zilch NODS, POINTS HIS THUMB to the large CHAPEL/MAUSOLEUM
complex near the ENTRANCE, and walks slowly back to the pit.

EXT/INT. CHAPEL COMPLEX/DARLA'S URN - MINUTES LATER

ESTABLISHING SHOTS: CLOSE ON - Metros STRIDING across the Pathway
of Remembrance through the Garden of Memory past an antique hearse,
ENTERS the arched CHAPEL NARTHEX, flanked by burial colonnades.
ANGLE ON - a PAIR of large Impressionistic surrealistic PAINTINGS,
similar but nonidentical sentinels, each depicting a personified soul walking
into the light. CLOSE ON - Intercutting the PAINTINGS to create a ghastly
feeling of "unheimlichkeit" from the doppelgänger effect, a prelude to the
Body Double. FOLLOWING Metros into the chapel, up the SPIRAL STAIRS,
into a dimly lit attic-like columbarium rotunda, where ashes and artifacts
are displayed in brass lockers with windows. ANGLE ON - a large DISPLAY
CASE with a life-size POSTER of Darla Darkcity mounted behind an URN of
her ashes; fresh-cut orchids, roses, lilies flank the sides; SYMPATHY CARDS
are jammed into the brass frame encircling the case.

ANGLE ON - Metros, VISIBLY SHAKING, as though the very thought
of murder makes him "claustrophobic," trapped in a world without virtue
and decency. INTERCUT - Metros STARES BACK AND FORTH between
the POSTER and the SCROLL, POCKETS the scroll; CLOSE ON - one
CARD stands out from all the others with red roses and bouquets: a solitary
flower - A BLUE DAHLIA. Metros PLUCKS the CARD and reads it aloud.

METROS
(shaking, reading)
"Dearest Darla, Your Death will be avenged by the
Ascension of the Art! With all my love, Manifesta."
(pauses, puzzled)
Manifesta?

CUT TO - EXT. CLOSE ON - Metros's PORSCHE, EXITING the scene. We hear impatient ENGINE GROWLS turn to high-pitched SCREAMS as he whips out of the driveway and down the "sainted" boulevard.

EXT/INT. SAG OFFICES/THE CASTING COUCH - DAY

Metros strolls past the gold letters "SCREEN ACTORS GUILD" and enters the Headquarters on Wilshire. He is BLOCKED by a sick, spiteful, officious DESKMAN, right out of Dostoyevsky.

                    METROS
          (politely)
     Good afternoon. I am inquiring into the whereabouts of
     an actress involved in a motion picture production that
     may or may not be legitimately sanctioned by the Screen
     Actors Guild.

               SPITEFUL DESKMAN
     If you aren't one of us, we will shut you down! Damned
     indie productions! If you don't let us paint your wagon, we
     won't let you roll with it!

                    METROS
     I didn't say that I have anything to do with an independent
     production company operating outside SAG-indie
     guidelines.

               SPITEFUL DESKMAN
     Well now. If you aren't <u>production</u> or <u>talent</u>, who the hell
     are you?

                    METROS
     I can't say. But I have information that relates to this so-
     called talent, and I need information in exchange.

               SPITEFUL DESKMAN
          (obviously frustrated)
     This had better be for real. I'm warning you.

(mumbles to himself)
We will drive you out … spend you out … wait you out …

The deskman PUNCHES buttons on the intercom, GESTURES "Up";
Metros moves on and UPWARD in the ELEVATOR to the next bureaucratic
level.

ANGLE ON - OFFICE DOOR, PLAQUE, "Scab Finders Group." Metros
opens the door and hesitates, taken aback by the "horrifying" view that
greets him but trying not to show it, but still unable to keep himself from
stopping and taking it all in.

NARRATOR, METROS (V.O.)
Aside from the leering, surgically damaged face of the
perfectly proportioned freakish "ideal" of femininity (no
doubt the masterpiece of a bevy of inept plastic surgeons)
staring at me from behind the executive desk, two other
things immediately offended me. The second was a large
number of diplomas, degrees, certificates, and licenses
spread across one wall. And the third was the scab
gallery -- head shot after head shot covering the remainder
of the walls, actors and actresses whose careers would end
before they'd begun.

For a moment I was at a loss. The leering face was so
obviously altered, so disturbingly unnatural. And the way
she was staring at me with her unnerving moue made
me think she wouldn't mind if we stood there staring at
each other forever. But I did mind. So I was glad when she
finally spoke, her voice both garish and provocative.

STATUESQUE LAWYER LADY
(corpulent lips moving)
Do come in, Dr. Metropolis. I am quite familiar with your
professional practice and your popular book of the lost
angels.

METROS
(nodding toward the doomed starlings'
photographs)
Nice gallery you have here. Are they all <u>Wanted Dead or
Alive</u>, or do they simply fade to black?

STATUESQUE LAWYER LADY
Any artist who won't sign with us will be denied
membership; and without membership they will never
work for a major studio. So in effect, you have answered
your own question -- they simply fade to black.

METROS
So, that's how it is? It sounds like a policy of blacklisting,
which seems rather paradoxical from the perspective of
Hollywood history, don't you think?

STATUESQUE LAWYER LADY
(her voice softening)
I'm not paid to think or to examine the ironies of history
and philosophy as you are, Dr. Metropolis. And by the
way, you're on our list as an unaffiliated indie author ...
or didn't you know that?

METROS
No, I didn't.

STATUESQUE LAWYER LADY
(motioning to a large couch)
Well, you are. But you are still welcome to sit here with me,
while I try to convince you to change your wicked ways ...

METROS seats himself on the couch.

STATUESQUE LAWYER LADY and her unnerving *moue* RISES from the
executive DESK, deftly crosses the room in black stiletto heels, CLOSES
and seductively LOCKS the OFFICE DOOR, and SEATS herself beside
Metros, her right hand placed firmly on his knee.

STATUESQUE LAWYER LADY (CONT'D)
I'm a great admirer of yours, Joe. May I call you Joe? It's not often I get to converse with a man of your prominence.
(moves her hand up his thigh)
The men around here are so small-minded -- so full of pomp without much circumstance. I long to meet a man of your caliber, Dr. Metropolis ... a man of your towering intellect.

METROS
(tries to slow her advances with his hand)
Ahem. I need your help in identifying an actress and her employer, who may be of mutual interest to us.

Metros REACHES into his jacket pocket for the SCROLL, and as he does, HER HAND begins to roam, moving slowly over his lap.

STATUESQUE LAWYER LADY
(seductively)
Yes, Joe. I can be a big help to you, that is, if I want to. I have a photographic memory and a knack for faces. Let me hold it, Joe. Let me see it. Let me have it, please.

Metros HANDS HER the rolled-up SCROLL, which she unfurls. ANGLE ON - the CROWD of FACES WATCHING from across the room; they appear to be STARING at his predicament.

NARRATOR, METROS (V.O.)
While she stared at the scroll, the Gallery of Faces stared at me. How many of them had been in this very same position? Filled with desire for something they needed, looking for help of some kind -- looks of longing, looks of confidence and composure, staring past all the uncomfortable realities. I suddenly felt uncomfortable with my position on the casting couch.

57

METROS
(struggling to be dignified)
Well? Can you help me or not? I don't have all day. I have places to go, things to do, people to talk to …

STATUESQUE LAWYER LADY
(pleading, seducing)
Don't be that way, Joe. Don't be unkind. I can help you find your mystery actress and her outlaw indie director, but you have to ask me nicely … Can you ask me nicely, Joe?

METROS
(diplomatically)
I'm sorry if I seem impatient. I don't mean to be rude, and I do appreciate your personal interest in my case. I'm flattered by your attention, but …

STATUESQUE LAWYER LADY
Then be flattered, Joe. Just be flattered. I'm a fervent admirer, Joe. Let me admire you in my own way …
(breasts heave in anticipation, face shines with wantonness)
Let me hold you, Joe. I want to feel the strength of a man I truly admire.

Metros CRINGES at that ghoulish deformed FACE, then steels himself. LIFTING HER HEAD with his fingers, he LOOKS DEEPLY, perspicuously, into the EYES of the WOMAN; beyond the ravages of time and inept surgeries, beyond the unattractive, is a desire to be beautiful, a timeless yearning to be loved.

METROS
(unbuckling his own belt)
I am truly flattered …

CLOSE ON – the casting couch. We can sense the pull of the gripping drama as the woman indulges herself, and Metros does not resist when the Lawyer Lady broaches the subject with refined feminine delectations.

ANGLE ON - the FACES on the WALLS are looking on; this time the faces are staring at Metros with STERN DISAPPROVAL -- desire, yes, but desire tinctured with ALARM. Metros STRAINS to maintain his composure, resolve stiffens. He lifts her head to a halt, this time with both his hands.

METROS (CONT'D)
I'm not sure I can allow this to continue … I'm beginning to feel somewhat used -- somewhat objectified!

STATUESQUE LAWYER LADY
You can stop me anytime you want, Joe. But then you won't get what you're looking for … I can give you what you want, Joe. I definitely have what you want. I know exactly what you want. But you won't get it without my help.

SMILING, reveling in Joe's predicament on her casting couch and his unbridled responses to the principle of the thing, she LEANS BACK, UNBUTTONS her white silk BLOUSE, UNCLIPS her black BRASSIERE, revealing nothing less than perfection of form and function. Her perfectly tanned body is sculpted, toned, and polished to an adamantine gleam. Below the neck, she is dazzling, she is astonishing. Metros is agog.

METROS
(nearly swooning)
You are so beautiful … so attractive … so desirable …
(convening the power of his manly imagination)
You look to my eyes as alluring as the Venus of Cyrene!

We realize (MATCH CUT) that the Venus of Cyrene is a classic "HEADLESS STATUE," without arms that needed either twisting or restraint. Metros LEANS forward toward the panting, provocative, perfectly Statuesque Lawyer Lady.

STATUESQUE LAWYER LADY
Then come to me, Joe, as you would come to a living, breathing goddess. Come to me, Joe, and join me in the enchanting theater of love.

EXT. CHATEAU MARMONT - EARLY EVENING

Metros PARKS on Havenhurst Drive, West Hollywood, and he CROSSES SUNSET in a jaywalking hurry. ESTABLISHING SHOTS: BILLBOARDS on SUNSET, the most notorious CHATEAU this side of perdition, the LOBBY ENTRANCE, where Metros THUMB-DIALS ...

> METROS
> (feigning confidence)
> Hello. My name is Joe. I know all about you and Manifesta, Scarlett. I'm downstairs in the lobby, waiting for you to join me for dinner. I'm tired and hungry, and I don't like to be kept waiting.

He doesn't have to wait long. FAVOR ON - SCARLETT, eyes hidden behind oversize SUNGLASSES, blonde hair cloistered under a big FLOPPY HAT; she is wearing a gold choker, a tailored blouse, and a tweed skirt, showing a lot of leg. She MOVES SLOWLY, as though pressure and tension were in the air.

> METROS (CONT'D)
> (without a hint of solicitude)
> Good evening, Scarlett. So nice of you to join me.

> SCARLETT
> (cheeky, hint of curiosity)
> You've got a lot of nerve coming here to threaten me. What are you, some kind of blackmailer? All I can say, Mister, is you've got a lot of nerve.

Metros presses close to Scarlett, speaking face-to-face.

> METROS
> I've got a lot of backstory on you too, Scarlett, which gives me, shall we say, the advantages of verisimilitude. Now, if you behave yourself and avoid making a cliché out of this scene, I'll treat you to a nice dinner, and I'll explain to you

my purpose and my nonthreatening agenda ... That is, unless you would prefer me to be threatening.

                    SCARLETT
          (indignant, then seductively, adjusting hat
          with both hands)
No, I would not! I just want you to know that I'm good at keeping secrets -- I mean, when I have to; I mean, when I want to.

                    METROS
I know exactly what you mean, Scarlett.

Metros places his arm around Scarlett's waist and ESCORTS HER into the intimate DINING ROOM: 1920s Prague-like ambiance, eternally chic, brocade walls, mirrors, antique lighting.

                    METROS (CONT'D)
          (tightening his squeeze)
Still, I intend to convince you that the dramatic revelation of secrets from the backstory is a very useful theme in narration. It goes as far back as Aristotle's Poetics.

                    SCARLETT
          (warming to his embrace)
Really? I didn't know that.

DISSOLVE TO - The DINING TABLE, where Metros is seen (not heard) explaining his mission to Scarlett. Scarlett appears to relax with the arrival of an arugula, shrimp, and blood orange salad. By a TIME CUT/ TRANSITION to the main course of the meal, THE COUPLE is now chatting away like old friends. TIME CUT - LIVE CONVERSATION.

                    METROS
You were saying that this Manifesta is some kind of mad genius of underground films, a budding auteur-extraordinaire?

                    SCARLETT

Oh, yes. She is exceedingly talented. She is a true
mastermind. Driven by dark passions, her personal vision
goes way beyond the beyond. We all love her.

                    METROS

And <u>who</u>, might I ask, is this <u>we</u>?

                    SCARLETT
                (giggling playfully)

The cast, silly. We're all staying at the Chateau Marmont
until the top secret shootings and public screenings are
over. It's all very hush-hush.

                    METROS
                (slyly, perceptively)

Which means you're just dying to tell me when and where
that would be …

                    SCARLETT

We're all supposed to meet on Friday night, at the corner
of Sunset and Londonderry, to witness <u>the happening</u>.

After Scarlett reveals these secret things, she reveals more than her charms.
CLOSE ON - Scarlett, removing the DARK SUNGLASSES and FLOPPY
HAT, displaying her BEAUTIFUL FACE: the <u>FACE of DARLA DARKCITY</u>.

CLOSE ON – Metros's REACTION: Metros is STUNNED by the physical
resemblance to Darla Darkcity, STUPEFIED by the philosophical "*imp of
the perverse*" that could have *murdered* such a raving beauty.

                SCARLETT (CONT'D)

Dr. Metropolis? Hello, Dr. Metropolis, this is your dinner
guest speaking. Earth to Dr. Metropolis!

METROS
(clearly bewildered)
I'm sorry, Scarlett. You look so much like Darla Darkcity,
I think you short-circuited my brain. How in the world
did they do this? This goes way beyond the art of makeup.

SCARLETT
Yes, Dr. Metropolis, this goes way beyond makeup. But
this is the kind of realism that Manifesta demands of her
actors and actresses.

METROS
You called me Dr. Metropolis … You know who I really am.

SCARLETT
(laughing)
You can't hide who you are any more than I can hide from
my new identity.

METROS
And I thought I was being clever.

SCARLETT
You are clever, Dr. Metropolis. And you understand actors.
That's how come we all know who you are. You don't think
we just read screenplays, do you?

METROS
No, I guess not. But I must say, I did enjoy playing the
hard-boiled detective with you.

SCARLETT
So did I, Doctor. I think I enjoyed your act almost as much
as you did.

METROS
                 (noticeably embarrassed)
You're just being kind. I admit I was having fun ... before
I knew exactly what, or rather whom, you look like. Now
I'm embarrassed by my own pretense.

                 SCARLETT
Don't be. If you want to know the truth, it's what we
actors do ...
Watch carefully now ...
                 (motions, conjuring the air with her hands)
Concentrate on the moment ... focus on the emotion ...
watch for it now ... wait for it ...
                 (places her hands flat on the table and leans
                 forward)
We pretend!

They BOTH LAUGH like children, wining and dining until a WAITER
finally arrives and presents the CHECK to Metros.

                 METROS
                 (signing for the bill)
Thank you for a lovely evening, Scarlett. I really can't
remember having so much fun ...
                 (looks up and smiles)
And don't worry; all your secrets are safe with me.

                 SCARLETT
                 (leans forward seductively)
But it doesn't have to end so soon, handsome. You know I
have my own room.

                 METROS
I relish the thought, pretty lady. However, it's too soon --
honestly, it is. But the next time I call you up, you can be
sure it's because of that smile of yours -- that smile I can
still feel in my hip pocket.

SCARLETT
(charming and inquisitive)
Fair enough, you dear, sweet man. But before you go, could
you do something for me?

Could you tell me <u>what kind of lost angel</u> I might be?

METROS
(cherishing the moment)
Hmmmm, let me think … You might be … you might
quite possibly be -- or at least you are well on your way to
becoming -- a fourth-order simulacrum.

SCARLETT
Sounds intriguing, Dr. Metropolis, but what does it mean?

METROS
(somewhat pretentiously)
I'm not sure we have the time --

SCARLETT
(motions impatiently)
I'll make time; no one is in a hurry in this magic castle, as
you can see. I want you to tell me <u>what kind of lost angel</u>
I might be, or becoming, or whatever.

Scarlett FLASHES Metros a SMILE -- a smile that fills a man's pockets yet
leaves his pretenses around his ankles.

METROS
Very well, Scarlett, since you put it that way. A fourth-
order simulacrum is a postmodern extension of a tradition
that goes back to Greek statuary, as far back as Plato's
cave. Basically, there are two kinds of image making. The
first is a faithful reproduction, a precise copy. The second
is intentionally distorted in proportion or scale to give
viewers an <u>appearance of correctness</u>, when it is, in reality,
a tad malformed.

SCARLETT
(her smile disappears)
So you think of me as malformed?

METROS
(pretenses down at ankles)
On the contrary, I find you incredibly attractive, incredibly provocative in every way. And that's what I'm getting at, if you would allow me, and if you would bring back that beautiful smile of yours ...
(satisfied, he continues)
The concept of the simulacrum is seen again in Nietzsche's Twilight of the Idols, where he argues that most modern philosophers tend to ignore reliable input of the senses, resorting instead to sophisticated --

SCARLETT
(cutting him off)
Can we move on to my lost angel, Dr. Metropolis -- the angel that I am becoming?

METROS
(clutching a shred of dignity)
Of course. You, my dear, are a construct of our modern times. You are not just a copy of the real; you are fast becoming a new reality, a truth in your own light. You are not just the embodiment of a historic reality; you are an angel of the hyperreal -- and a beauteous angel at that.

SCARLETT
(flushed with appreciation)
Oh, Dr. Metropolis, tell me more.

METROS
(gingerly, counting fingers)
Of the four orders of simulacrum, as in likeness or similarity, we have covered three -- one, the reflection of reality; two, the perversion of reality; and three, pretense,

66

which we, or rather you, already know all about. Should we stop there, Scarlett, with the simple art of pretense? Do you want me to stop there?

SCARLETT
(rolling her head gracefully)
No! No! Don't stop. Keep going. I find your thoughts strangely exciting -- so different from the tawdry scripts we're assaulted with. Please continue.

METROS
The purpose of my philosophical meandering is to set the mood, in modern terms, while the real thrust of my discourse is to introduce you to the bold and naked potentiality of the <u>fourth-order simulacrum</u>.

SCARLETT
(eyes closed in anticipation)
Yes … yes … introduce me.

METROS
Frankly, Scarlett, you're not real; you're <u>hyperreal</u>. You create an entirely new reality -- with your own premises, your own rules, your own value systems. You are no more real than Main Street in Disneyland, no more real than <u>Westworld</u> or <u>Jurassic Park</u>.
(noticing Scarlett wince)
But I want to assure you, my dear, that the fourth-order simulacrum plays a very important role in our modern world. Far from the distractions of a contrived fantasy world, I believe that you are involved in an epic drama that only you, and people attuned to what you represent, are capable of arousing.

SCARLETT
(wide-eyed with rising urgency)
Yes, that's it exactly. Don't you dare stop now!

METROS
(with mounting puissance)
Unlike Nietzsche and Baudrillard -- who view such simulations in negative terms -- I agree with Gillies Deleuze, who examines favorably and ultimately treasures the avenging angel of the hyperreal!

Scarlett leans forward, rapt with expectation, as Metros delicately encircles her face with his fingertips.

METROS (CONT'D)
For it is in appreciating her sublime _dramatic beauty_ -- in grasping the vast potentiality of her social function -- that we find an avenue by which _dubious yet accepted ideals_ and _privileged positions_ of society can be challenged and overturned!
(clasping both her hands)
In situations like this, it is the very fondness for you, the very striving for you -- the overarching _idea of such a beauty_ -- that can be redeeming!

Scarlett SHUDDERS. Warming to the solace of the aesthetics, she literally BEAMS with a bright, self-satisfied SMILE.

SCARLETT
Now that's my kind of philosopher! Is there any more where that came from?

METROS
(rising to leave)
You find a way to introduce me to this mysterious Manifesta on Friday night, and I'll see what I can do.

EXT. SUNSET BOULEVARD/TECH-NOIR - FRIDAY NIGHT

ANGLE ON - METROS, watching a CROWD ARRIVING, GATHERING, spilling out onto the BOULEVARD, STOPPING TRAFFIC, swelling with a sense of urgency and anticipation; CAR DOORS FLY OPEN. Metros attempts to retreat but is swept out into the street. CLOSE ON - his PANIC in the MADDING CROWD; CLOSE-UP - a human HAND, soft and warm, finds his in the midst of the dark chaos.

SCARLETT
(whispering into his ear)
Hello, handsome.

Scarlett, with that unforgettable SMILE, those oversize SUNGLASSES and big FLOPPY HAT, stands so close Metros can inhale her lovely perfume as they wait for the show to go on.

We hear a wave of RAISED VOICES, as great plumes of SMOKE, LIGHTS rise from the seams of an ALLEYWAY in the foreground. Captivated by the growing spectacle, the CROWD SURGES out; GRIDLOCK ensues; awestruck PASSENGERS join mass confusion.

Scarlett TURNS and THROWS HER ARMS around Metros to avoid being swept away in the MADDING CROWD. A moment caught in SLOW-MOTION: her FACE turned upward to his … LIPS pressed together in desiderium … BODIES not separate but united as one.

THE MADDING CROWD
(counting down in accordance with the LASER LIGHTS flashing onto the blank BILLBOARD WALL)
Ten! Nine! Eight! Seven! Six! …

DISEMBODIED SOUND EFFECTS
(loudspeakers blasting)
Resonating BASE TONES! Followed by piercing, high-pitched SCREECHES!

THE MADDING CROWD
… Three! Two! One! Zero!

The name MANIFESTA suddenly appears on the WALL, accompanied by an earsplitting high-frequency SOUND of such clarity it makes neck hairs bristle, followed by a thunderous BOOMING BASS; all chest cavities vibrate within a three-block radius.

Metros HOLDS Scarlett close, with HIS HANDS tightly on HER HIPS. The aurora theatricalis of the TECH-NOIR BEGINS with near-holographic imagery: ANGLE ON – the makeshift screen. We see a confrontation between TWO MEN; a WOMAN frantically SHRIEKS - vivid, unmistakably recognizable characters of a familiar double murder mystery played out on the back steps of a Westside condo. The sense of actuality is mesmerizing: A KNIFE swipes the air; the UNARMED MAN takes a defensive stance; everyone on "The Strip" tenses; the WOMAN cries out to distract the ATTACKER, to no avail. Young women in the audience cry out, young men clamor in protest; but the crowd cannot prevent the SLASHING, the point-blank STABBINGS of the man, the SEVERING of the woman's head, as violent hatred finds its mark.

And then, the snuff movie is over; the civic amphitheater is once again bathed in the blinking, flashing semidarkness of the city street, the Sunset Strip on a typical Friday night.

                    SCARLETT
              (strolling with Metros)
        What do you think of my new boss now?

                    METROS
              (obviously affected)
        I am more anxious than ever to meet him, I mean, her.

                    SCARLETT
        Well, tonight's your lucky night, big boy. Are you sure
        you're up for it?

                    METROS
              (squeezing Scarlett's hand)
        You bet I am.

70

SCARLETT
(bumping his side)
I have to warn you, though. She's not like anyone you've ever met before.

METROS
Thanks for the warning, sweetheart. From what we witnessed tonight, I wouldn't expect her to be like anyone else on this planet.

SCARLETT
(pulling Metros forward)
In that case, you'll find her waiting for us at the private after-party -- it's right down the street.

INT. NIGHTCLUB ON THE SUNSET STRIP - LATER

Squeezing past two burly BOUNCERS, the COUPLE ENTERS the inner sanctum of the private AFTER-PARTY: DARKNESS cloaks; STAGE LIGHTS reveal; LIVE MUSIC issues; DANCING seduces - men with men, women with women, men with women - HEADS MOVING in a hyperesthetic trance to the deep, pounding, primordial ROCK RHYTHMS from the STAGE. FAVOR ON - The COUPLE finds the BAR.

SCARLETT
(softly, into his ear)
You're on your own, handsome. I'm not invited. You'll have to tell me all about it later.

A HOSTESS escorts Metros away from the LIVE MUSIC/DANCING past a line of BOOTHS filled with nouveau cinema society and LA hipsters deep in conversation, to a private VIP TABLE, where MANIFESTA is holding court. The decor is totally KETCHUP: framed pictures of ketchup bottles, tomatoes, splattered ketchup; red lights overhead, red napkins, etc.

CLOSE ON - MANIFESTA, a striking woman with beautiful Asian features wearing a low-cut, sleeveless, backless evening gown that leaves little if any of her exquisite feminine contours to the imagination -- the color of the fabric is ketchup red. Her hair is black and shining, a weave of bloodred ribbons, waves of sensual tresses that barely touch her shoulders.

CLOSER ANGLE - HER FACE, delicate and narrow, with dramatic eyebrows, high cheekbones, and naturally succulent lips; her right EYE is OPENED conspicuously WIDE with a MONOCLE. Her radiant beauty is, in a word, painful. This kind of beauty simply beckons to be admired -- were it not for the painful realization that she is LOOKING STRAIGHT AT YOU and probably RIGHT THROUGH YOU, with a blazing preternaturally OPENED EYE.

                         METROS
                   (at a loss for words)
              I had no idea.

                         MANIFESTA
              You were expecting Ayn Rand perhaps?

                         METROS
              Well, yes. I mean, no. I don't know exactly what I mean.

                         MANIFESTA
              Well, that's a start. A shred of honesty goes a long way
              with me.

Manifesta GESTURES for Metros to be seated with a wave of an empty CIGARETTE HOLDER. Still, she places it between her lips and scrutinizes Metros with her piercing MONOCLED EYE.

                         METROS
              Now that you mention it, there is a strong similarity
              between you and her, between your eyes and hers, as I
              remember them. That is, Ayn Rand's eyes, I mean.

                         MANIFESTA
              Yes ...
                   (expecting him to continue)

METROS

If you'll forgive me, her eyes had that same unrelenting intensity as yours, that same unnerving quality -- at least I find it unnerving. It's as if a penetrating intelligence were being communicated, along with a disarming sternness that serves as a warning against frivolousness.

MANIFESTA

Well, well, Dr. Metropolis, perhaps you deserve your reputation after all. Actually, I'm flattered. Because Ayn Rand was truly a beautiful woman, a triumphant champion of human dignity, and an intellectual of the first degree. I like to think that my work in the cinematic arts is an extension of her objectivist philosophy ... an extension of her strident morality into the visual arts.

METROS

How so?

MANIFESTA

As you know, Ayn based her philosophy on objective reality -- on man's reason -- not on whims, articles of faith, or chauvinistic edicts. Furthermore ...
> (adjusting the length of the empty cigarette holder)

... Ayn deplored the collective use of force, coercion, entitlements that devalue human dignity. I like to think that I -- with my latest brand of cinema verité -- am extending her banners to an ultramodern feminism.
> (adjusting precisely again)

By extending my cameras and computers into the sinister corners of these masculine abominations -- as an avatar of truth -- I am erecting a bulwark of direct existential experience, exposing the violence against women that has run rampant in this town far too long.

METROS
(appreciatively)
You certainly exposed something tonight. There is no denying that. I've never experienced anything like it, in terms of my own visceral responses.

MANIFESTA
(with piercing vision)
Tonight I exposed the cowardly male ego, which hides behind celebrity, group psychology, and male chauvinism, while it denies a modern woman the dignity of her own free will. Tonight I exposed Hollywood's and society's hatred of modern women for what it is -- <u>violent and self-righteous envy of her liberated sexuality</u>.

METROS
(struggling for composure)
I'm not sure I would go that far ...

MANIFESTA
No, of course, you wouldn't, Mr. Philosopher to the Stars. But someone has to! And apparently that someone has to be a women who knows what it's like to be a woman -- a woman with passionate convictions and vision.

Metros simply NODS, attempting to withstand the relentless glare of Manifesta's monomaniacal exposé.

MANIFESTA (CONT'D)
(repositioning the monocle)
I consider myself to be a champion of justice. And there has been no justice for beautiful women in this town, only exploitation, contempt, and violence ...
(cheeks flushed, gaze intense, shimmering with a crimson hue)
Where there is no justice, there is violence! And I for one intend to bring these revelations of man's violence against women <u>out of the closet and into the streets</u>!

74

METROS
(attempts to respond)
Bravo, Manifesta --

MANIFESTA
(cutting him off)
I am creating a new myth for society -- the Myth of the Eternal Rerun -- and I intend to rerun this theme of Man's Violence Against Women with increasing levels of realism until no one can escape the veracity of the direct physical experience!

When Manifesta finishes speaking, she LEANS gracefully BACK, exposing an abundance of FEMALE PULCHRITUDE, fiery red PLUMES set against the milky whiteness of the leather upholstery.

METROS
(flustered)
I clearly see what you mean ... Ummm ... I can fully appreciate the social value of a feminist provocateur ...
(struggling to concentrate)
I happen to share your repugnance for the exploitation of beautiful women ...
(obviously distracted)
Actually, I consider myself to be an advocate of women's rights ...

CLOSE ON - MANIFESTA, who is "SEEING" (OBIE LIGHT) right through Metro's wandering thoughts, as though they were completely transparent. She LEANS FULLY FORWARD again, exposing the delectable fullness of her TWO PERFECT BREASTS, and gives Metros a good hard mono-monocular SQUINT ...

Metros assumes the posture and appearance of a deer caught in the headlights.

MANIFESTA

And would your responses be exactly the same if the dearly departed Ayn Rand were here in this same dress staring at you in the face?

MATCH CUT/FLASHBACK TO - the VENUS OF CYRENE / BACK TO - Manifesta's FEMALE PULCHRITUDE / BACK TO - the VENUS OF CYRENE / BACK TO - Manifesta's FEMALE PULCHRITUDE / BACK TO - METROS EMBARRASSED, CHASTENED by his own masculine responses to the headless STATUE and the immediate eye-pleasing, mouthwatering beauty-before-him vis-à-vis the eternal beauty of the lofty philosophical propositions under discussion.

METROS
(embarrassed, chastened)
I'm afraid I see your point all too well. I mean, I truly "see" your point, Manifesta. I am beginning to realize that any attempt to weasel out of this would be futile, and I would probably end up hating myself in the morning.

MANIFESTA
(victorious, then candid)
Finally, a philosopher who refuses to argue against a painful reality -- there might be some hope for mankind yet! Seriously, Dr. Metropolis, Kaltrina and I both know who you are working for, and we both know why you wanted to see me tonight ...
(picks up a tomato and a Sharpie, begins writing)
Please come to our new home in the Pacific Palisades, and we'll help you solve your pathetic case!

Metros RISES TO LEAVE, Manifesta HANDS him the large ripe red TOMATO with an ADDRESS -- freshly scripted with a Sharpie -- on the surface of its otherwise flawless skin. Metros RETURNS to the BAR, where Scarlett is waiting, nursing a Bloody Mary.

METROS
(tomato in hand)
Anyone who endeavors to argue with your boss had best
be prepared to lose.

SCARLETT
(sipping the Bloody Mary)
Really, darling, how did it go?

METROS
(fondling the tomato)
Frankly, Scarlett, I made a damn fool of myself.

SCARLETT
Don't worry about it, handsome. I'm sure others have done
much worse.

We FOLLOW the COUPLE to the DANCE FLOOR, just in time for a SLOW
DANCE number; they DANCE among the MOVING DMX LIGHTS.
Scarlett flashes Metros a SMILE that stays with a man, as she CONSOLES
HIM with the supreme confidence of a real live ANGEL on the DANCE
FLOOR. The slow dance comes to an end. CLOSE ON - SCARLETT
whispering in Metros's ear.

SCARLETT (CONT'D)
Lucky you, Dr. Metropolis. You get to take me home.

INT. CHATEAU MARMONT/SCARLETT'S BEDROOM - NEXT DAY

In BED, the morning after, Metros is STARING at Scarlett, who is still
sleeping, naked beneath the sheets. Her EYES OPEN.

METROS
Good morning, Scarlett. You open your eyes, and my sun
also rises.

SCARLETT

(yawning, smiling)

You're sweet. I bet you say that to all your lost angels. Really, darling, what did you think of <u>Mani's new reality</u>?

METROS

It awes me and scares me at the same time -- like I was watching the violent birth of a brilliant new star. Her movie trailer was tech-noir at its very best -- not black, but luminous. The <u>fear</u> that she creates is <u>not a fear of technology</u> but a fear of what <u>dark forces lie simmering within ourselves</u>.

SCARLETT

(blithely)

Did you notice the reactions of the crowd? Do you remember how it felt?

METROS

Yes, we were all sickened to our very souls: people were swooning as blood and tears were falling faintly through the universe. Like the descent of the last curtain of the last picture show -- it fell upon the living and the dead.

SCARLETT

(cheerfully)

My death scene is <u>coming soon</u>, ya know?

METROS

(mildly dismissive)

I don't even want to think about that.

SCARLETT

(playfully indignant, pulling the coverlets higher up)

That's not fair! You're only thinking of me as a warm body double, when you're really fixated on the <u>drama and the death of Darla Darkcity</u>.

METROS
(assuring, seductive)
<u>Au contraire, ma cherie</u>. I'm not interested in the angel you
are striving to become. I am completely smitten with the
angel that you are.

They EMBRACE, passionately, as though it were the first time.

INT. METROS'S OFFICE - DAY

Metros ENTERS, converses with Holly at her desk.

HOLLY
(chewing gum)
Well, it's about time. I was beginning to think something
might have happened to you.

METROS
(leaning on Holly's desk)
Thanks; only good things so far.

HOLLY
You do look rather pleased with yourself, Doc -- a little too
pleased. BTW, how are you doing with the latest tycoon
case? You know, he keeps calling to ask me why you aren't
answering your phone.

METROS
(riffling through the mail)
Too soon to tell. Anything else?

HOLLY
Yeah, the Repo Man needs the Porsche back in a hurry,
like yesterday …

METROS
(handing her the keys)
Did he say anything else?

HOLLY
(casually)
Yeah, he said you'll have to make do with a Ferrari for a while.

METROS
(simply nods his approval)
I was wondering, does the name Manifesta mean anything to you?

HOLLY
Not personally, why?

METROS
She's a feminist provocateur who's taken cinema verité to a whole new level. I know it's not politically correct, but I was wondering about her sexual orientation.

HOLLY
You know me, Doc. I don't ask. I don't tell.

METROS
(gives Holly a quizzical look)
Well, if Manifesta is indeed a lesbian, she is definitely one of the most beautiful lesbians in the world.

HOLLY
Great. And what do you want me to tell Mr. Zero Vaynilovich when he calls again?

METROS
(deliberating)
What do you say to a man named Zilch, when all you've got is nothing?

EXT. PACIFIC PALISADES/FERRARI CALIFORNIA - SUNSET

TIME LAPSE - the BIG ORANGE BALL moves in the sky; hesitates for a moment in "*illud tempus*" before stepping off the ledge of the HORIZON, leaving the world DARKER by the minute/second. ANGLE ON - A FERRARI CALIFORNIA motors along the PALISADES.

INT. PACIFIC PALISADES/MANIFESTA'S HOUSE - EARLY EVENING

The nearly new azure-blue FERRARI CALIFORNIA comes to a STOP on Paseo Miramar; Metros dismounts the "Prancing Horse" and APPROACHES a modernist HILLSIDE GEM: spotlights illuminate the meticulous landscape; the FRONT DOOR has been left OPEN.

Metros enters the INTERIOR - a post and beam structure, with emphasis on the HORIZONTAL stagelike composition; linear beams, walls of glass, expanses of varnished ceilings; floors -- obsidian tiles, as black as a director's clapboard; modern furniture -- refined minimalism, creating a play of space and light and unobstructed VIEWS of Los Angeles after dark. We FOCUS ON - Metros's POV, moving INTO THE ROOM to check out the city lights; a SHADOWY FIGURE flashes by the open PATIO DOOR.

MANIFESTA'S VOICE (O.S.)
It would be better if you would come and sit over here by the fire.

Indeed, there is a SITTING AREA and a FAUX FIRE -- flickering in high definition on a large FLAT-PANEL display. Manifesta, wearing tight black jeans and an even tighter black T-shirt, SEATS HERSELF, splendidly, in a beige leather CHAIR.

METROS
(looking back to the window)
Better for what? I was beginning to enjoy the view.

MANIFESTA
(directing Metros to a chair)
Better for us to talk, Dr. Metropolis. Better for us to talk about Zero Vaynilovich for one thing ... Better for us to talk about Kaltrina Dahl for another.

METROS

Was that Kaltrina Dahl I just saw climbing out of the swimming pool? And were those feathers she was wearing?

MANIFESTA

Kaltrina may join us sooner or later, depending on how she feels at the time.

METROS

Okay, if you say so. I'm just happy you agreed to see me again … on behalf of my client, of course.

MANIFESTA

Of course.

Metros notices that Manifesta is still clutching the empty CIGARETTE HOLDER, but she is not sporting the MONOCLE. He pensively considers a remote possibility that this particular object of auspicious and distinctive attire might actually be the MISSING/STOLEN OBJECT that Zilch had mentioned.

BEGIN FLASHBACK – HOLLYWOOD FOREVER. We see Zilch groping around in Byron Harmsway's coffin, with Metros looking on.

END FLASHBACK.

METROS
(probing the possibility)
I noticed that you aren't wearing a monocle this evening?

MANIFESTA

You mean the monocle. And no, I only wear it when I create my art films.

METROS
(rhetorically, yet not entirely satisfied with her answer)
Is that so?

MANIFESTA
(waxing indignant)
Yes, Dr. Metropolis, it is so. And you can ask me anything you like about my artistic creations, but nothing will be gained by probing into my personal effects.

METROS
Well, it is part of my commission to gain access into the ultimate source of your inspiration -- artistically speaking, that is.
(shifting his direct approach)
I was wondering if you share any developmental continuities with that fellow Kristophalus. You know, that guy who goes around covering things up with curtains, ostensibly in an effort to reveal them. Isn't he manifesting the same kind of public art as you are?

MANIFESTA
(with rising contempt)
Oh, please! You disappoint me, philosophically speaking, that is! Don't even think about grouping me, my source of inspiration, or my art films with that machismo miscreant! We have absolutely nothing in common!
(her womanly visage glowing ever more brightly)
You, of all people, should be able to look into the origins of his inspiration as easily as a Freudian psychotherapist can look into the developmental psychology of a hysteric.
(frowns with disapproval)
And if you bothered to look, you would see the male perversity at its base. You would see, in his early works, the attempts to constrain the female figure -- the binding ropes, the high-tensile fabrics, the intricate knots -- the obvious sadist aesthetic should be as clear to you as the so-called artistry of Japanese bondage pornography!

METROS
(agreeably)
Now that you mention it, there is an element of <u>obsession</u> in his modus operandi; an obsession to wreak havoc upon sacred monuments, as well as a <u>compulsion</u> to recruit an aggressive undercurrent of <u>social complicity</u> through bureaucratic channels ...

MANIFESTA
That's correct! The shame is that the <u>bureaucratic complicity is applauded</u> -- the circles of political, capitalistic, pseudo-artistic "good old boys" live out their domineering fantasies in public -- and they do so, in this town, to the detriment of femininity itself.

METROS
(striving for common ground)
I sympathize with your position, Manifesta. I myself am both emotionally and professionally set against the <u>victimization of the female</u>, as it is historically, and often tragically, played out in this town.

MANIFESTA
(with rising indignation)
Well then, why not <u>philosophically</u>, Mr. Philosopher to the Stars? What are you waiting for? Don't you realize that this is the very <u>crux of the matter</u> ... the crux of the drama that you have been sent like an <u>errand boy</u> to find ... the crux of the "MacGuffin" depicting the essence of creativity that Zero Vaynilovich now lacks?

METROS
(charming in defeat)
If I agree with the social criticism of the gifted feminist provocateur, does the <u>errand boy</u> receive a small gratuity to take back to the <u>grocery clerk</u>?

MANIFESTA

You amuse me, Dr. Metropolis, and that's quite rare in this business.

METROS
(striving to bridge a gap)
Isn't it time you called me Joe?

MANIFESTA
(condescending)
I really don't think so, Dr. Metropolis. While I do sense some redeeming qualities in your boyish sincerity and absence of malice, it is my experience that such familiarity invariably breeds contempt!

Amid the posturing, an attractive, engaging, and arresting WOMAN'S VOICE literally FLOATS ("REVERB") into the room.

KALTRINA DAHL'S VOICE (O.S.)
(maternal, reverberating)
"Now, now, Manifesta, the man did ask you nicely, even humbly, in my opinion. Dr. Metropolis has managed to endure your caustic diatribe, and he deserves the same respect from you that you would ask of him."

Kaltrina's disembodied VOICE is soft and cool, the ROOM is clear and bright, but SHE's NOT THERE. Metros RISES abruptly; Manifesta RISES more gracefully, arms crossed; Metros WALKS toward the PATIO DOOR.

KALTRINA DAHL'S VOICE (O.S.) (CONT'D)
(this time with urgency)
Please stop right there, Dr. Metropolis. Please don't try to come any closer!

METROS
(stopping in his tracks)
Why in the world not?

                    MANIFESTA
              (scornfully, shaking her head)
She is afraid that you will fall in love with her … They
always do.

There is no answer; only a soft RUSTLING SOUND that can be heard
coming from the unlit DARKNESS of the POOL AREA.

                 MANIFESTA (CONT'D)
              (arms crossed under breasts)
Modesty forbids.

                    METROS
              (turning in a circle)
But you told me, or implied, you would <u>both</u> help me to
solve my case …

              KALTRINA DAHL'S VOICE (O.S.)
              (patiently, explanatory)
A historical romance is what it is; my fondness for Zero
Vaynilovich is what it is; my appreciation for the many
motion pictures we made together is, and shall always be,
enchanting.

Metros stands amazed; Manifesta grows increasingly impatient.

                    METROS
              (thinking about Zilch)
On behalf of my client, I need to ask you about a <u>stolen
object</u>, Kaltrina. I don't mean to accuse you or offend you
in any way, but it has been relayed to me in those terms …

              KALTRINA DAHL'S VOICE (O.S.)
              (firmly, resonating)
You can tell Sad-Zero that I know very well what he wants.
More importantly, you can tell him that I am also acutely
aware of what he currently lacks!

METROS
(waxing Aristotelian)
Might I suggest a form of compromise … in an effort
to moderate the discord … as a desirable attribute of
beauty … as an approach to restoring harmony?

KALTRINA DAHL'S VOICE (O.S.)
(more firmly declarative)
If you insist on asserting the utility of your philosophical
imperatives, I can tell you: The sorrow of said Zero is that he
has lost his perspective! Moreover, the very thing that Zero
needs most is soon to arrive via the Metrolink Train. Tell Zero
he can find his lost perspective one week from tomorrow at
precisely six o'clock in the morning at the Glendale Station.
(charmingly, politely)
Now, if you will excuse me, Joseph, it's time for me to
change into my evening attire and get ready for my lofty
bedtime adventures.

METROS
(sarcastically, to the shadows)
I'd say it's been nice meeting you, Kaltrina … but since
we haven't actually met yet, I'll just say that it's hard to
say good-bye.

MANIFESTA
(equally sarcastic)
Truer words have never been spoken.
(feigning a yawn)
Now, if there isn't anything more we can do for you, Dr.
Metropolis, I'm feeling rather tired myself.

Manifesta ESCORTS Metros to EXIT via the FRONT DOOR.

METROS
(entreating, at the threshold)
I know it's asking a lot, under the circumstances, but I
need more!

(holding the door open)
If it wouldn't be too much trouble ... if you could find it
in your heart ... I am fascinated by your hyperreal cinema
verité -- your passion to the point of provocation ... your
emotional drive to reveal the truth!

MANIFESTA
(hands Metros a metal token)
Here's a token for <u>Angel's Flight, The World's Shortest
Railway</u>. I'll try to make some time for you on location.

EXT. ANGEL'S FLIGHT RAILWAY/DOWNTOWN LA - DAY

ESTABLISHING SHOTS: ANGLE ON - arched Hill Street ENTRANCE;
SIGN, "Angel's Flight"; the steeply inclined TRACKS leading to the Upper
VICTORIAN STATION; the CALIFORNIA PLAZA situated atop Bunker
Hill. CLOSE ON - Manifesta, in black jeans and sheer black chiffon, busy
with a PRODUCTION CREW (Engineer Bees) setting up booms, reflectors,
and assorted high-tech paraphernalia on the TRAIN TRACKS.

METROS
(leans over railing, shouts)
Thanks for the pleasure of watching the hottest new
filmmaker in town!

Manifesta SIGNALS with her HAND, and a LASER LIGHT beams onto
the TRACKS. She NODS to an ENGINEER BEE, who turns off the laser
beam. Manifesta CLIMBS up to the LANDING where Metros is waiting;
the view is PANORAMIC. We see she is wearing the MONOCLE among
sequins of sweat.

MANIFESTA
(approaches Metros)
As long as you don't confuse me with any other directors
in this town, I'll allow you to stay. You know I'm nothing
like them, and I don't ever want to be.

(eyes Metros confidently)
You shouldn't presume that I want to break some kind of glass ceiling for the sake of sexism. Sexism is simply not my style -- in fact, I find the subject of sexism to be uninteresting.

METROS

How can you separate your radical brand of feminism from the trappings of sexism? Aren't they two sides of the same coin?

MANIFESTA
(over the sounds of the city)
Hardly. I do not intend to blaze a path that other, lesser individuals can easily follow. I admire leaders, not followers, no matter what their sex is. It will take leaders with indomitable courage to challenge the prevailing macho aristocracy. My work in digital compositing and cinematic art raises the bar higher than ever before, with a bold challenge and a warning to men and women alike -- that the Charities, the goddesses of beauty and creativity, favor the most deserving!

METROS

I assume you are referring to the Gratiae, or Graces, in Roman terms.

MANIFESTA

Absolutely.
(suddenly distracted)
No, no, not there! Wait! I'll be right down.

Manifesta DESCENDS the platform to adjust some ELECTRONIC EQUIPMENT. She BEAMS a LASER LIGHT to a point on the side of an ADJACENT BUILDING, EYES some readings, WRITES down some calculations, SIGNALS an ENGINEER BEE, RETURNS to the DECK.

MANIFESTA (CONT'D)
You're still here?

METROS
May I ask what kind of spectacle you are creating here,
Manifesta?

MANIFESTA
(sequins of sweat glistening)
Well, if you promise to tell no one in advance: it's a new
project designed to shatter the stereotype of the damsel
in distress. By placing naked starlets on these tracks --
holographically, like phantoms in the night -- I plan to
capture modern man's primal reactions in high-definition.

METROS
Goodness, that sounds intense! I promise to keep your
secret from all but two, the first being my client.

MANIFESTA
No problem. Zero Vaynilovich is much too proud to even
recognize my work, let alone interfere.
(signaling her minions to carry on with a
fluttering wave of her hand)
And who is this second person that you simply must
inform?

METROS
Actually she's one of yours. Her name is Scarlett, your
body double for Darla Darkcity.

MANIFESTA
Oh, she already knows. They all do. Everyone in the artistic
avant-garde is intimately connected, don't you know?
And Scarlett, the brave girl, will always be welcome by
my lamplights.

METROS
(sincere distress showing)
I realize all too well the tragic necessity of your work. And I admire the courage and conviction it takes to confront such ugly truths. It's just that the degree of realism you create is so disturbing -- and I am becoming so fond of Scarlett, personally -- that I am not sure I can even bear to watch the scene of her murder.

MANIFESTA
(obviously pleased, adjusts the monocle, quips)
Silly rabbit ... my "Trix" are for your kids.

Stunned by the brilliance of a finer future that just flashed before his eyes, Metros GRABS the metal RAILING for support. CLOSE ON – Manifesta smiling.

NARRATOR, METROS (V.O.)
Suddenly I got it! I realized that Manifesta is not just another up-and-coming director in the entertainment industry, not just a flash-in-the-pan shock jock of modern cinema. It finally occurred to me that she had taken it upon herself with great passion to confront an unacceptable evil in our society with conscientious force -- to change our modern world. "Your death will be avenged by the ascension of the art"; here was the battle cry of a feminist provocateur, who would use her vivid powers of persuasion to make a better world for our children than the one we inhabit today.

ANGLE-ON – Metros still HANGING ON to the railing at Angel's Flight.

METROS
(visibly shaken)
It's brilliant! Brilliant!
(regaining his composure)
Your "treatment" of these illusory corpses gives me the creeps ... but now that I understand your intentions, I wouldn't miss it for the world.

FOCUS ON - an AIRLINER, descending to LAX, passing over the LA SKYLINE. CLOSER ANGLE - we FOLLOW/FADE into the SKY.

INT. COSMOPOLITAN STUDIOS/EDITING SUITE - NEXT DAY

Zilch is SEATED at a deluxe EDITING CONSOLE: Tiers of CONTROLS, VIDEO DISPLAYS, and a flat-panel BIG SCREEN beam overhead. ANGLE ON - WATERFALL SCENES: Last of the Mohicans (with D. D. Lewis), We're No Angels (with R. De Niro, S. Penn), Niagara trailer (Marilyn Monroe). ANGLE ON - Metros ENTERS, escorted by a PA. Zilch RAISES HIS HAND, concentrating, preventing interruption. WATERFALLS are seen on all the displays.

> ZILCH
> (concentrating)
> I'll be with you in a minute. I'm just finishing up a montage
> for Byron Harmsway's digital video memorial.

> METROS
> (watching the waterfalls)
> These watery images are beautiful.

> ZILCH
> (concentrating, adjusting)
> A master cinematographer paints the screen with both
> forms and shadows: umbra, darkness, and light are colors
> too. I was serious when I told you I strive to see more
> clearly in the dark.

> METROS
> (watching the screens, sees cinematic
> waterfalls, different men are falling in
> slow-motion)
> What's the theme?

                    ZILCH
          (moving the Niagara trailer to the big screen
          overhead)
Falling!

                    METROS
Just falling?

                    ZILCH
          (adjusting the controls)
No … not just falling … falling with style!

WORDS are shown ON-SCREEN at the start of the NIAGARA TRAILER. The blaring MUSIC is concurrent with the WORDS: "Niagara" … "And … Marilyn Monroe … as the Tantalizing Temptress … whose Kisses fired men's souls!" MARILYN SINGS … The Niagara Trailer Narrator begins (V.O.): "She sang of love, just as she lived for love, like a Lorelei, flaunting her charms as she lured men on and on to their eternal destruction …" ANGLE ON - Zilch, SILENCING the SOUND; as the Niagara trailer continues, dramatic film noir SCENES are "playing" OVERHEAD.

DISSOLVE (to show the passage of time) - from the BIG SCREEN, BACK TO - the EDITING CONSOLE; several spectacular WATERFALLS are seen LOOPING on the SCREENS. ANGLE ON - Metros, who is now SEATED, and Zilch, who is TURNED SIDEWAYS from the video screens and the editing console, facing Metros.

                    ZILCH (CONT'D)
          Let me get this straight. You've been on the job all this
          time, and all you've got to show for yourself are two dead
          bodies, a disfigured statue, eyewitness accounts of an
          unsolved murder, shaky evidence of a second murder plot,
          accusations of a serial sadist on the loose, and rumors
          of famous starlets scheduled to be tied buck naked to a
          railroad track?

METROS

Yes, that's about it.

ZILCH

Some kinda detective you are.

METROS

But, Mr. Zilch, I'm not a detective, and I never advertised myself as such. I am a philosophical counselor, and you engaged me to --

ZILCH

I know why the hell I hired you, Metropolis. It's just that I'm getting desperate, and I was expecting more from you, something more insightful, perhaps.

METROS

Well, I did have a brief Socratic dialogue with Kaltrina Dahl, in which she discussed your previous history and her interest in your films. Moreover, I encouraged her to meet you in person in an attempt to find some common ground.

ZILCH

You mean you actually saw her?

METROS

Well, not actually.

ZILCH

What do you mean not actually? Did you see her or didn't you?

METROS

Before I try to answer that, could you tell me if she likes to wear feathers?

ZILCH
(shuffling some papers, DVDs)
Why, yes. She certainly does.

METROS
(curious)
Does she wear these feathers all the time?

ZILCH
(stops shuffling)
No. Not at nighttime, of course. What are you getting at?

METROS
Well then, yes. I do think I saw her. I saw her briefly, that is.

ZILCH
(impatiently)
Well, if you saw her briefly, how in the hell did you manage to have a conversation with her about our relationship and our reconciliation?

METROS
I think you would call it voice-over.

ZILCH
(angry, crumpling papers)
And where was the nouveau notorious Manifesta when you were having this voice-over conversation with my Dahlia?
(threatening, snaps a DVD)
And if you tell me how beautiful this presumed lesbian is one more time, I'll ... I'll ... I'll ...

METROS
Calm down, Mr. Zilch. Philosophy teaches that all beings before us have created something beyond themselves -- as you have with your films. The only question you need

to answer for yourself at the moment is this: <u>Would you rather go back to the beast than surpass the man</u>?

                    ZILCH
          (clenching fists)
I would rather have my darling Kaltrina back. With her help, I could surpass the lesbian!

Zilch POUNDS his FISTS on the CONSOLE with such force that the video display SCREENS jump to DISTORTION and STATIC.

                    METROS
Look here, Mr. Zilch. I'm just beginning to get a handle on this case.
          (standing, as to leave)
I have gained certain insights from Byron Harmsway -- may he rest in peace -- and from Kaltrina Dahl herself. I am not sufficiently informed as to offer you a working hypothesis at this point.
          (straightening his jacket)
However, I believe it may come down to the underlying values and attitudes you hold dear; and I promise -- if you give me enough time to approach Kaltrina Dahl on her own terms -- I will get to the rock bottom of this mystery.

                    ZILCH
          (resigned, his head slumps)
Your search for answers sure takes a long time. But what other choice have I got?

                    METROS
There's one more thing: Kaltrina told me to tell you that the very thing you are <u>missing</u> will arrive by train in Los Angeles next Wednesday. She told me you would find what you are looking for at the railway station in Glendale at six o'clock in the morning.

ZILCH
(brightening, as with the dawn)
Why didn't you say so? This is exactly what I have been waiting for! It may not be the love of my life, but it's a step in the right direction!
(stands, pumps Metros's hand)
I'll pick you up at your seedy office on my way to the Glendale station. Meanwhile, I expect you to work on solving this case every waking hour -- and remember, time is of the essence!

INT. METROS'S OFFICE / SCARLETT'S DRESSING ROOM - EVENING

INTERCUT BETWEEN - METROS/SCARLETT. Metros sits at his desk; the office is empty and dark except for the small desk lamp. He looks lonely. He pulls out his cell phone and dials, a few beats, then, Scarlett answers. She is in a bustling DRESSING ROOM; in the MIRROR, we see her in DARLA DARKCITY regalia.

METROS
Hey, beautiful, when do I get to see you again?

SCARLETT
(giggles)
Oh, my dashing philosopher. How does tomorrow evening sound? I'm almost done with the last of my pickups.

METROS
Pickups? Are you trying to break my heart already?

SCARLETT
Really, daahhling! A pickup is when a scene is filmed after the principal photography has been completed ...
(tweaking her eye makeup)
Manifesta wants my untimely death scene to be perfect in every way. Don't you want my death scene to be perfect?

METROS
(gushing with sincerity)
You know I can't bear the thought of you being "shot" --
ex post facto or otherwise. But I get it, Scarlett ... really
I do ... and I applaud your artistic intentions; I realize
that you and Manifesta are literally striving to do <u>Darla
Darkcity</u> justice.

SCARLETT
(smiling into the mirror)
That's my philosopher, and my hero!

METROS
Am I anything else to you?

SCARLETT
And my lover!
(cupping the cell phone for privacy)
If all goes well, we'll be having a cast wrap party tomorrow
at sundown at Shutters on the Beach, and I want you to
celebrate the ending with me.

METROS
(earnestly)
Some part of me is already there!

EXT/INT. SHUTTERS HOTEL/WRAP PARTY - NEXT EVENING

ANGLE ON - Metros EASING the convertible FERRARI into the
cobblestone DRIVEWAY of the fashionable beach resort HOTEL.

CUT TO - METROS'S POV as he ENTERS the posh LOBBY-LOUNGE,
which is jam-packed with the multifarious CAST sprawled among the
elegant SOFAS and chic antique CHAIRS. The WRAP PARTY is in full
swing. Looking for Scarlett, Metros wanders through crowded SALONS and
decked-out DINING ROOMS of the luxurious Santa Monica beachfront
resort. CLOSE ON - SCARLETT: wearing a svelte black jacket over a short

black dress, she looks ravishing -- just like Darla Darkcity on her final date. Scarlett approaches Metros; her lips brush against his cheek.

SCARLETT

What kind of angel do you see in me now, Dr. Metropolis?

METROS

Do you really want me to answer that question?

SCARLETT

Yes, silly … or I wouldn't have asked.

METROS

(grasping both of her hands)
I see an angel to have and to hold.

Scarlett BLUSHES and LOOKS AWAY. Metros DROPS HER HANDS and looks seriously DEJECTED. Realizing this, Scarlett GRABS HIS HANDS and PLACES THEM firmly on her HIPS and says:

SCARLETT

You give up much too easy. And that wouldn't be any fun at all!

Scarlett TURNS and WALKS theatrically, attractively past a DINING AREA and up to a large OPEN BAR, as Metros catches up.

METROS

(hungrily)
Don't you want to catch some dinner tonight? That seafood looks delicious.

SCARLETT

(playfully, handing Metros a flute of champagne)
An actress always has to watch her figure, daahhling …
Or no one else will want to!

METROS
(raises the glass)
A toast, then, to hunger and beauty!

Scarlett LAUGHS; she PULLS Metros toward an EXIT that leads through an outdoor terrace to the paved beachside PROMENADE. The sun has set; a dusky twilight lingers as darkness falls.

EXT. BEACHSIDE PROMENADE - CONTINUOUS

ESTABLISHING SHOTS: the darkening COASTLINE; PALM TREES buffeted by the balmy Pacific BREEZES; the carnival lights and Ferris wheel of the Santa Monica PIER in the background. ANGLE ON - Scarlett and Metros STROLL the beachside promenade.

SCARLETT
(still sipping champagne)
Why so quiet, handsome? It's such a sexy evening -- so full of promise and dramatic potential. Are you angry with me for playing hard to get?

METROS
Angry? No ... It's not you, Scarlett. It's a client that I'm awfully worried about. He's got lots of obvious issues, which are common enough in this town. But I'm not sure that I can help him -- in the way that he expects me to.

SCARLETT
(smiling, teasing)
Really? You mean it? My brilliant, passionate intellectual is at a loss?

METROS
(stopping; nursing his drink)
Yeah. You might say that. But the code of patient confidentiality forbids me to discuss my professional consultations openly.

SCARLETT
(taking his half-empty glass)
Poor dear. Maybe I can help ... I want you to forget about
the man you can't talk about ... I want you to use your
imagination to create a super-objective -- or driving
force -- of a new play!

METROS
Really, Scarlett, I don't think ...

SCARLETT
Don't argue with me, lover; I don't want you to think; I
want action! I want you to create a new object that you
can identify with ... and an active verb that captures the
drama.
(handing back his glass)
Here! Bottom's up! And don't say a word until you can
give me "the object" and "the action" -- pure and simple.

METROS
(empties the glass and hands it back to her)
All that comes to my mind is the image of a supermassive
star that is about to collapse!

SCARLETT
(stifling a giggle)
Good! Very good! Now explain, in fifty words or less,
exactly what this image of a collapsing star means to
you ...

METROS
(hands pressing in animation)
When a great star expends its source material, it begins to
lose its outward radiance ... It can no longer forge any new
elements ... It starts to collapse, as its gravity outweighs
its radiance!

(an exploding gesture)
But that's not all … The collapsing star "explodes" -- its death has such dramatic force that precious metals like gold are created … as stardust!

                    SCARLETT
          (smiling in the lamplight)
Your fifty words are up, Dr. Metropolis … But I must say, you have an extremely adorable mind.

Scarlett DROPS both GLASSES into the sand; they enter into a passionate KISS as the FERRIS WHEEL of the PIER slowly turns and the shimmer of CARNIVAL LIGHTS wink on in the distance.

INT. SCARLETT'S ROOM, SHUTTERS HOTEL - CONTINUOUS

We see the same CARNIVAL LIGHTS from a different POV: The COUPLE is LYING partially dressed on the BED. Scarlett, in her black dress, is nestled under his arm. Metros, his shirt opened wide, is GAZING out the WINDOW at the ocean view.

                    SCARLETT
          (snuggling)
You know you make me happy.

                    METROS
          (caressing her)
And you put stardust in my mind.

                    SCARLETT
It's called method acting, daahhling. Did it help? Really?

                    METROS
I think so.
          (beat)
But I was hoping to speak with Manifesta again tonight. And I was hoping to meet Kaltrina Dahl. Somehow, she holds the key.

SCARLETT

Oh, they have already been and gone. This party is just for the cast and the production crew. With those two, it's always the next big thing.

METROS

(fretfully)

That's too bad. It's tragic, really. I don't know what to do now, or how to help my client, the collapsing star.

SCARLETT

(looking directly at him)

Now don't take this the wrong way, handsome, but remember when I told you I like it when you play the hard-boiled detective with me? You know, the hard guy who will stop at nothing to get to the hidden truth. A knight-errant on the mean streets of Los Angeles ... A man who is not himself mean, but is tough and persistent and adventurous ... and very good in bed.

METROS

Are you trying to tell me something?

SCARLETT

I'm just trying to give you a clue, daahhling: about me ... about women ... about your collapsing star of a client and this troublesome case!

METROS

Huhhh?

SCARLETT

(playfully mounting him, waving arms as in flight)

I happen to know that Manifesta and Kaltrina took several members of the production crew away from the party tonight. And, if you were interested -- as a hard-boiled detective would be -- you might be able to squeeze some information about their "location" out of this <u>beautiful winged angel</u> who, as you can see, is <u>flying high above you</u> ...

METROS
(perplexed, then suddenly)
Angel's Flight! They're at Angel's Flight tonight?

Metros JUMPS UP out of bed and quickly DRESSES, as Scarlett LOOKS ON in amusement. He SITS on the BED to tie his shoes. We hear the LAUGHTER and MUSIC coming from the wrap party.

METROS (CONT'D)
(hurrying, at the door)
I've gotta go, Scarlett. How can I thank you? Will you be all right?

SCARLETT
Don't worry about me, daahhling. I've got lots of friends waiting for me downstairs ... I'm sure we're going to be partying all night long.

EXT. ANGEL'S FLIGHT RAILWAY - LATER THAT NIGHT

We see Metros PARKING the TOPLESS FERRARI on Hill Street, near the base of the ANGEL'S FLIGHT inclined railway. ANGLE ON - Metros POV: We see the BOARDING AREA and steep TRACKS that run uphill to the California Plaza STATION. CLOSE ON - a PLATFORM approximately midway up the tracks: we can see a BEAUTIFUL WOMAN (Kaltrina Dahl) on the dimly lit PLATFORM; we can see Manifesta LOOKING ON from the adjacent STAIRS; we can see the DP, KEY GRIP, and GAFFER readying some HMI LIGHTS.

CUT TO - Metros EXITING the Ferrari and SLEUTHING unseen up to the COLUMN of the Angel's Flight ARCHWAY; he observes the following ACTION: The HMI PARS are switched ON; The BEAUTIFUL WOMAN in a glamorous ostrich-feather dress experiences a WARDROBE FAILURE -- she stands demurely, elegantly aloof, as she gracefully wraps her arms in front of her breasts and lowers herself into a sitting position with the grace of a ballet dancer. PULL FOCUS - Metros looks on in amazement contemplating the ACTION.

EXT/INT. PACIFIC COAST HWY / METROS DRIVING - NEXT MORNING

Metros is DRIVING the Ferrari California along the scenic Pacific Coast Highway. He TURNS into the parking area of Will Rogers State Beach, THUMB-DIALS Scarlett, and SETS his SMARTPHONE to speaker.

INTERCUT BETWEEN - METROS/SCARLETT. Metros is seated in the FERRARI, looking out to sea; Scarlett is under the bedsheets.

                    METROS
          Good morning, beautiful.

                    SCARLETT
          (still groggy from sleep and partying, and etc.)
          You left without saying good-bye.

                    METROS
          I was feeling so good, I decided to take the long way to my
          office … and I didn't want to wake you.

                    SCARLETT
          (less groggy)
          Then why are you waking me up now?

                    METROS
          I just couldn't help it. And besides, I wanted to thank you
          for helping me out with this tragic case of mine.

                    SCARLETT
          So, you got your money's worth at the Angel's Flight
          Railway?

METROS
(with heart on sleeve)
I got some insights is all I can say. But the real reason I
called is not just to thank you, but to tell you that I can't
wait to see you again.

SCARLETT
(artfully reserved)
Is that so?

METROS
Yes, it is. It is definitely, enthusiastically, undeniably so.

SCARLETT
Okay, daahhling. I have to be available for Manifesta
during postproduction -- just in case. But let's see ... I've
got something exciting going on tomorrow night with
some friends at the Wax Museum. Can you meet me there
at precisely ten o'clock?

METROS
(suddenly beaming)
Of course. Tomorrow night it is.

EXT/INT. HOLLYWOOD WAX MUSEUM - NIGHT

ESTABLISHING SHOTS - Hollywood and Highland Center: SIDEWALK,
"Walk of Fame" from Kodak Theater to Hollywood and Highland; STARS
underfoot; a chorus of TOURISTS; real, live DISNEY CHARACTERS
glide up escalators, down stairs; a life-size TYRANNOSAURUS REX
devours a CLOCK above the RIPLEY'S "Believe It or Not" Odditorium,
reminding us "time is of the essence." Metros, ARRIVES at the double-
arched ENTRANCE of the WAX MUSEUM, looks around, checks his
watch, decides to ENTER ...

INTERIOR, among scads of WAXEN CELEBRITIES, new and departed,
Metros FINDS Scarlett arrayed as DARLA DARKCITY on a shadowy

STAIRCASE; she is striving (poorly) to remain motionless. ANGLE ON -
Metros moves up close, examines female anatomy:

> SCARLETT
> (scolding, whispers, like a ventriloquist to a
> dummy)
> Don't make me laugh while I'm method acting.

> METROS
> I was just admiring your costume, among other items …
> The only thing wrong with your methods, from my point
> of view, is there is no one else here but me to enjoy them.

> SCARLETT
> (still whispering)
> That makes no difference to me in the least. A true actress
> can perform the same, regardless of the circumstances.

Metros LOOKS around the ill-lit room: SEES a full house, to be sure,
but wax figures are not the most appreciative of audiences. Just then, we
HEAR a COMMOTION from the adjacent room: many LOUD VOICES,
all talking at once.

> SCARLETT (CONT'D)
> (ventriloquist's warning)
> Hush now. Don't you dare give me away.

The vociferous VOICES DRAW NEARER; a retinue of BUSINESSMEN in
well-tailored suits; backslapping jocularity, tasteless dialogue/vulgarity -- a
gaggle of assistant movie producers.

> SCARLETT (CONT'D)
> (whispers)
> Kiss me now.

Metros, being nonchalant, oblivious, only SHRUGS.

SCARLETT (CONT'D)
(whispers louder)
Kiss me quick.

METROS
(not getting it, whispers back)
I don't understand …

SCARLETT
(indignant, louder)
What part of kiss me don't you understand?

Like an actor who just realized he missed his cue, Metros EMBRACES
the nearly-motionless mannequin; KISSES her MOUTH, her NECK, her
BREASTS, like a teenager at a drive-in movie.

Suddenly, two "waxy" KEYSTONE COPS on the STAIRCASE "come to
life" and, rather roughly, give Metros the BUM'S RUSH down and out on
to the STARRY SIDEWALK of HOLLYWOOD BOULEVARD.

METROS
Wait! Stop! Stop! What are you doing?

KEYSTONE COP
(excitedly)
We're helping Scarlett to get discovered! And you were
really great as the fall guy!

The Keystone Cops REENTER the Wax Museum, leaving Metros on the
sidewalk among the "fallen stars."

EXT. WILSHIRE BOULEVARD/SCARLETT'S TECH-NOIR - FRIDAY
NIGHT

METROS'S POV - We see a CROWD GATHERING at Wilshire and
Westwood for a public debut of Manifesta's latest TECH-NOIR, Starring
DARLA DARKCITY, viewed from an alienating distance this time, with
Metros, the fall guy, looking on as an outsider.

ANGLE ON - the obtuse angles of the surrounding OFFICE BUILDINGS create an ARENA: The CROWD GATHERS, blocks traffic as before; HELICOPTERS CIRCLE. PULL BACK to METROS'S POV - distant, removed. We see LIGHTS; NUMBERS COUNTING DOWN; The name MANIFESTA; we HEAR the SCREECHING, RESONATING SOUNDS. Metros STANDS and WATCHES long enough to see the image of DARLA DARKCITY emerge from a LIMO and walk toward a LOOMING MANSION. He TURNS AWAY and WALKS THE WALK of a lonely guy:

NARRATOR, METROS (V.O.)
There is no mercy ... not in this town. You come here hoping that you might spend <u>one more night</u> in the arms of an angel ... But hoping is not the stuff of philosophy. Neither is wishful thinking. Scarlett is somewhere in that crowd with her new assistant movie producer. I just know it. I don't even have to see it. Pessimism is more reliable when it comes to human nature.

We HEAR the "CLAMOR of the CROWD" in the BACKGROUND.

NARRATOR, METROS (V.O.) (CONT'D)
Perhaps if I were a better man, I would have been able to take her in my arms and convince her <u>not to go there</u>.

A SHOT rings out, echoing in the night. Metros SHUDDERS. He WALKS ON; TURNING onto a DARK STREET, he sees a disheveled HOMELESS GUY -- with shopping cart -- lighting a CIGARETTE. Metros walks over, hands the man a twenty-dollar bill; The HOMELESS GUY SHAKES OUT a cigarette, HANDS IT to Metros, and LIGHTS IT for him. Metros continues to WALK THE WALK of a lonely guy, a lonely guy out on a night like this.

NARRATOR, METROS (V.O.) (CONT'D)
Being "perspicuous" is no picnic ... not in this town; not when all you see is cruel and hard and vicious. On a night like this, it feels like it should rain, but you know it's only the marine layer oozing in. On a night like this, you want to pull the darkness around you like a blanket, but

somehow the metaphor of a blanket is lost in the heat of the hot summer night.
> (takes a drag, flips butt)

On a night like this, you smoke, and flip the spent butt ahead of you, and watch it arc to the pavement and fizzle out with one last wink ... What's this?

ANGLE ON - Metros BENDS DOWN to investigate the glowing head of the cigarette, dislodged from the shaft. CLOSE ON - GLOW.

NARRATOR, METROS (V.O.) (CONT'D)
> (watching embers fade to black)

I should've known this would happen. It's here before my eyes like a memento -- a dying ember of an angel that is gradually disappearing from my sight.

INT. ZILCH'S LIMO - LOS FELIZ BLVD - EARLY MORNING

Inside the LIMO, Zilch and Metros are talking; DRIVER drives.

ZILCH
> (handing Metros a steaming cup of Starbucks coffee)

Are you certain Kaltrina said it would arrive on the 6:00 a.m. train?

METROS

I am certain about the time, the place, and the train. What I am not certain about is the exact nature of either the subject or the indefinite object you are seeking.

ZILCH

Leave that to me. I told you it was personal, and it is ... very.

METROS
(sipping coffee)
Would you like me to tell you what I've learned about
Manifesta's new reality-based cinematography?

ZILCH
(dismissing the topic)
I'm still in the movie business, Metropolis. I can't afford
any acute bouts of reality.

They DRIVE ON in silence, SIPPING COFFEE through lid slits.

EXT. GLENDALE TRAIN STATION PLATFORM - MINUTES LATER

ESTABLISHING SHOTS - Business as usual at the Mission-style
GLENDALE TRAIN STATION: The limo moves off to park behind the
Greyhound BUSES. On the RAISED PLATFORM amid LA COMMUTERS,
Zilch PACES the WALKWAY, looking for the commuter TRAIN(S).

Metros, who is STANDING near Zilch, LOOKS down the TRACKS toward
Los Angeles, where he notices a SPORT UTILITY VEHICLE DRIVE
ONTO, and STOP between, the two sets of RAILROAD TRACKS.

METROS
(curious and alarmed)
Do you see that? That SUV just stopped ... on the tracks! ...
It just stopped moving!

ZILCH
(stops pacing, stares)
I'll be damned. It's stopped all right.

NARRATOR, METROS (V.O.)
By this time, other people on the platform were beginning
to notice what was happening. And as they did, they began
to yell and shout. Indeed, there were doctors, lawyers,
mechanics, civil engineers, captains of industry, people of
every nation, race, and creed in Los Angeles in attendance.

And their outcries were transformed into a collective roar
of might around me. Yet there was nothing any of us could
do to mitigate the current stasis and its impending disaster.

ANGLE ON – The platform, with the SUV in the distance. FOCUS ON –
Metros and Zilch facing each other, panicked.

> METROS
> This is dreadful! It's not normal. It's not decent. This is a
> terrifying example of the stasis!

> ZILCH
> (growing increasingly frantic)
> What's with this <u>stasis</u>? Do you think it means something?

> METROS
> Look! A man is getting out of the SUV! He's getting out!

We can HEAR the SOUNDS of TRAINS APPROACHING. We can SEE
them coming in the DISTANCE. The YELLS, SHOUTS grow louder.

> ZILCH
> (grabbing Metropolis)
> It looks like he's getting out to watch! But what is he
> watching?

> METROS
> (trains approaching)
> It's <u>stasis</u>! He's watching the <u>stasis</u>!

> ZILCH
> (makes a director's frame on the SUV as
> trains approach)
> What's with this <u>freakin' stasis</u>?

> METROS
> (declarative)
> Stasis in the arts is tantamount!

ZILCH

Stasis in the arts is tantamount to what? Speak, man! Out with it!

METROS
(nearly shouting)
Stasis in the arts is tantamount to death!

ZILCH
(hand framing the shot as the trains collide)
I can see it! It's right here! It's here in every frame ...

TWO double-deck COMMUTER TRAINS, both alike in gravity, yet moving in opposite directions. ONE would normally slow to a stop at the STATION; the OTHER would pass on by in the blink of an eye. But today they are FUSED in a horrific TRAIN CRASH. VIEWED in SLOW-agonizing-MOTION, Zilch sees clearly the faces of the passengers through the WINDOWS -- passengers who are completely unaware of the STALLED SUV, the meaning of the STASIS, and/or the SPECTACLE that they are now a part of; unaware of annihilating fate that is about to come to pass. The CROWD on the platform STEPS BACK en masse.

In the midst of the commotion, the SHRIEKS, and the CRASHING, Metros realizes that Zilch is no longer standing beside him. Metros WHIRLS AROUND to look for Zilch, only to find the man COLLAPSED on the PLATFORM in a heap. Metros BENDS DOWN ... Suspecting a heart attack, he FEELS FOR THE PULSE, LOOKS UP, panicked.

INT. LIMO - EN ROUTE TO QUEEN OF ANGELS - MINUTES LATER

The DRIVER, white knuckles at the wheel, CAREENS WILDLY from the Glendale Station through Los Feliz -- great plumes of thick BLACK SMOKE from the train wreck can be seen through REARVIEW WINDOW. Metros, tossed about in the backseat, is BENT OVER SIDEWAYS, attempting to apply CPR to an unconscious Zilch.

EXT. QUEEN OF ANGELS - EMERGENCY ENTRANCE - MINUTES LATER

The LIMO SWERVES into the ENTRANCE of the QUEEN OF ANGELS HOSPITAL, barely missing two AMBULANCES (dispatched to the crash scene). DISSOLVE TO - the same location, where an unconscious Zilch is being ROLLED INSIDE on a gurney with O_2 and IV lines in place. An EMT GUY directs the LIMO DRIVER to clear out; Metros WAVES to the DRIVER, APPROACHES the EMT.

METROS

I know for sure that there are many more injured on the way. I wish there was something I could do to help.

EMT GUY
(consoling)
It's good you got here when you did -- it might be just in time. Looks like he might make it. But just in case, you'll want to have his loved ones close by.

INT. METROS'S OFFICE - DAY

Metros BURSTS IN, breathless from his walk up the hill (from hospital to seedy office). Holly is SEATED at her usual DESK.

HOLLY
(curious, stands up)
What's wrong?

METROS
(panting, breathing hard)
There is an axiom ... of predicate calculus ... that states that the number of city blocks one can run without stopping ... is inversely proportional to the number of cigarettes one has smoked in a day.

HOLLY
I thought you quit smoking, Doc?

We FOCUS on Metros as he STUMBLES into his INNER OFFICE and dumps himself into his CHAIR. Holly FOLLOWS, perches on DESK.

HOLLY (CONT'D)
(over SIREN in the background)
What's all the commotion? Is there another wildfire in
Griffith Park?

METROS
No, Holly, it's not just a fire … it's much worse. Everything
has come to a screeching halt!

HOLLY
(gets up, looks out the window)
Everything?

METROS
(bewildered)
The SUV … the trains … Zilch's heart! Everything! I don't
know what to do.

HOLLY
Well, let me cheer you up with some good news. I did some
investigating on my own for ya, Doc. And I got the latest
scoop on Manifesta -- in fact, she's the talk of the town.
(seating herself on the desk)
Her little exhibitions are getting worldwide attention --
everyone is duly disturbed -- there are calls for trials and
retrials, just like the old days …

METROS
(shaking his head)
You don't understand, Holly. Everything has come to a
<u>catastrophic stop</u>!

HOLLY
Not everything, Doc. She's an up-and-coming item in this
town -- a real phenom -- a legend in her own time.

METROS
(harshly, excited)
Holly, you're not listening! There's been a terrible train crash ... and I'm not sure that Zilch will survive!

HOLLY
(suddenly sentient)
You mean you just happened to put Zero Vaynilovich ... your client, "the latest tycoon" ... on a train that just crashed? How did you manage that?

METROS
He wasn't on the train! He was just part of the stasis ... and now he's in the hospital, and he may not make it, and I don't even know how to contact his family ...
(begins pacing)
I don't know what to do, Holly. I don't know where or who to turn to.

HOLLY
I don't know if this will help or not, but I do know something about men. In my humble opinion, you should cherchez la femme, Doc. Cherchez la femme! When in doubt of the emotions and motivations of a man, it's always best to look to the woman ...

METROS
(bolts up, revived)
That's it, Holly!
(kisses her on the cheek)
You're a peach!
(and hurries out)

EXT. PACIFIC PALISADES/FERRARI CALIFORNIA - DAY

We see Metros DRIVING hard with the top down; ARRIVING at MANIFESTA'S HOME: the front DOOR is locked; a FENCE prevents ingress from the sides; a SWOOP of SEABIRDS emerge, fly off.

METROS
(desperate, he dials)
Answer, Scarlett … answer!

INTERCUT BETWEEN - METROS/SCARLETT. Metros STANDS beside the FERRARI. Scarlett, in bikini, SUNBATHING in a LOUNGE CHAIR.

SCARLETT
Hello, handsome.

METROS
(bravely, withholding jealousy)
Hello, angel. I need you to do me a favor, if it wouldn't be too much trouble.

SCARLETT
I liked you better when you played the hard guy for me … I mean, with me.

METROS
(heroically restrained)
You're the one who dropped the ball, my lost angel. It was never up to me.

SCARLETT
Well, then, why are you calling me now?

METROS
Actually, I need to know where Manifesta is right now! It's really urgent, Scarlett … a matter of life and death, really! I can't explain it to you. I barely understand it myself. It's not for me is all I can tell you. Even if you don't take me seriously, please take this situation seriously. It's a matter of dramatic necessity!

                          SCARLETT
Well, why didn't you say so, handsome? She's at the
Hollywood Bowl as we speak … she's setting up one of
her magical cinematic creations.

                          METROS
                    (striving for distance)
Thank you, Scarlett. You're a pal.

                          SCARLETT
While we're on the phone, there is one thing I'd like you
to know.

                          METROS
                 (swallows, bracing himself)
Yeah, what is it?

                          SCARLETT
I really enjoyed our last kiss.

And then the connection GOES DEAD.

EXT. HOLLYWOOD BOWL / MANIFESTA'S SETUP - DAY

ESTABLISHING SHOTS: Long shot of the iconic AMPHITHEATER in its
naturalistic setting, seen from the cheap seats. ANGLE ON - the QUEEN
BEE (Manifesta), ON STAGE, directing her HIVE of ENGINEER BEES.
CLOSER ON - Metros is PARKING (Offstage-Right), WALKING IN
(Stage-Right), and STANDING in front of the APRON.

                          MANIFESTA
                    (sarcastically, to the gaffer)
Get ready to "strike the blonde," BB, it's the philosopher
to the stars!
                    (speaking down from the stage)
What brings you here?

                            METROS
                  (speaking loudly, projecting)
Haven't you heard? There's been a terrible accident ... a
train crash at the Glendale Station! It's pandemonium!
Sheer pandemonium! But that's not why I'm here. I need to
speak with you about Kaltrina Dahl ... I think that Zilch
may be dying!

                          MANIFESTA
Okay, you have five minutes.

Manifesta STRIDES across the STAGE, EXITS Stage-Left, and DIRECTS
Metros up to the outdoor TABLES of the Rooftop Grill. Manifesta
SIGNALS; coffee and croissants are promptly served.

                            METROS
                    (waiting for her to sit)
May I ask what kind of performance you are planning for
the Bowl?

                          MANIFESTA
It's the debut of my virtual avatar -- a tribute to dead
poets and composers. While the audience is listening to
the words and music, my virtual avatars will bring the
original artists back to life.

                            METROS
You mean you're going to project images of great composers
in midair like the frightening alter ego of the original
Wizard of Oz?

                          MANIFESTA
                  (gracefully sipping coffee)
Something like that ... but I have added a few more
dimensions.

METROS
(matter-of-factly)
Not to mention that you have nearly done away with "the man behind the curtain."

Manifesta reaches into the pocket of her skintight jeans and slowly withdraws a braided thread -- attached to a MONOCLE, which finds its way into her right EYE SOCKET (OBIE LIGHT).

METROS (CONT'D)
Look, what I really came here to see you about -- what I really want -- is to get you to help me, to help Zilch!

MANIFESTA
(eyeing Metros suspiciously)
And how do you suggest I could do that?

METROS
(emphatically)
By convincing Kaltrina Dahl to see him again ... before it's too late!

MANIFESTA
I might have known. You men are always so predictable.

METROS
Predictable or not, can you really deny the contributions that men like Zilch made to the art of cinema and American culture. Can't you cut him some slack?

MANIFESTA
(leans forward, eyes flaring)
It's not my job to appreciate the past, but to overcome the present! Once upon a time, there were real conflicts, real causes worth fighting for. Then along comes a generation of auteurs waving their undeveloped antlers at the silver screens -- with a nostalgic pantomime of antiquated heroism that is acted out ad nauseum. The "captive

audience" is entertained, maybe even impressed, but it is seldom captivated, rarely enervated, and almost never elevated!

(adjusting the glaring monocle)

Men like Zilch gave us commercial entertainment as a substitute for real life, and neither men nor women are the better for it. Why should I cut him any slack?

METROS

(struggling against the glare, paraphrasing Albert Einstein)

To widen our circle of compassion to embrace all living creatures, perhaps?

MANIFESTA

If you must hurl petty bromides at me, I prefer the soaring thoughts of Ralph Waldo Emerson, who was much more emancipating than Mr. Einstein … And I quote: But a compassion for that which is not and cannot be useful and lovely, is degrading and futile.

METROS

(munching a butter croissant)

I'm not quite sure what you -- or even Emerson -- might mean by the term useful …

(cringing at the thought)

Surely you don't mean practical as in pragmatism?

MANIFESTA

(rising, with indignation)

Not pragmatism, Dr. Metropolis, activism! Useful and lovely activism! And now, if you'll excuse me, I must get back to my work!

Manifesta STARTS to leave. Metros STANDS and FOLLOWS her.

METROS
(desperate, trying for sympathy)
I get it, Manifesta ... I appreciate your passionate cultural agenda, I really do. <u>But you are the influential filmmaker now</u>! And you, of all people, should know what kind of power Zilch once wielded ... how much he has lost in his fall from grace ... and how little he has left to defend himself with!

MANIFESTA
(confronting Metros fiercely, glaring at him face-to-face)
I understand men like Zilch all too well, Dr. Metropolis. What I want to know -- and I mean this seriously -- is what does Zero's loss of power and grace have to do with you?

METROS
(standing his ground)
He's my client, for goodness' sake. It's my job to help him; it's my profession!

MANIFESTA
That's a charming work ethic you have there, Dr. Metropolis, but it's not the whole truth, and you know it!

METROS
But why are you interested in me? Why do you even care about my motivations?

MANIFESTA
(discreetly removing monocle)
I have my reasons.

The ARGUMENT is interrupted by a PYROTECHNIST BEE.

PYROTECHNIST BEE
I'm sorry to interrupt, but we need to gauge the flux of the pyrotechnics to match the luminous output of the CGI.

MANIFESTA
(sternly, competently)
Are you certain we'll have enough comets and fountains
for the main performance, as well as the encore?

PYROTECHNIST BEE
Yes, boss, we have lots and lots of all the specified devices.

MANIFESTA
(dismissing the worker bee)
Good. I'll be right there.

Metros, having returned to his chair on the Rooftop Grill, LOOKS UP at
Manifesta with his head in his hand, supported by his elbow on the table.
Manifesta SPINS her chair around backward and SITS IMPATIENTLY, as
though anxious to leave.

METROS
You're going to test the fireworks in broad daylight? Don't
you have to wait until dark?

MANIFESTA
Light … dark … it's all relative to the source. It all depends
on the intensity of the source. I thought you, of all people,
would know that!

METROS
(with candor befitting)
No, Manifesta. You're wrong about me. I never claim to have all
the answers. A philosopher is not defined by what he knows …
but what he loves … and sometimes, who he cares for.

MANIFESTA
(looking Metros over, sans the monocle, she
drops her guard)
Very well, Mr. Philosopher, you win! I won't stand in your
way. You can try to convince Kaltrina Dahl yourself --
sometime around midnight tonight.

EXT. PANORAMIC RECAP TO THE SEA - SUNSET TO DARK

AERIAL TRACKING SHOT - east to west: the smoking CRASH SCENE; HOSPITAL/Observatory; HOLLYWOOD SIGN, HILLS; SUN setting/Set.

INT. MANIFESTA'S HOUSE / FLASHBACK SEQUENCE - MIDNIGHT

ANGLE ON - the FRONT DOOR has been left OPEN, as before. Metros ENTERS the modernistic masterpiece; there appears to be no one home. The FIRE is flickering silently on the FLAT SCREEN. The beige CHAIRS are empty. REFLECTIONS of the EMPTINESS WITHIN and the city LIGHTS BEYOND, depending on the angle of the strategic spotlighting. Metros is drawn to the pool area by SOUNDS of SPLASHING, determined to investigate.

METROS
(switching on the light switch)
Heavens!

There, APPEARING before his eyes, glistening in the soft glow of the PATIO LIGHTS, is an astonishing VISION OF LOVELINESS: ANGLE ON - Kaltrina Dahl: ARISING from the steps of the SWIMMING POOL with the grace of a goddess incarnate, in what appears to have once been a white leotard, but was now moistened to the point of sheer invisibility, revealing every voluptuous curve of her exquisite form, every delectable nook, every evocative furrow and line that nature has drawn upon the body of a woman who was arising now from the most mysterious of waters, whose limpid fingers seemed reluctant to release her from their grasp. This vision of loveliness is clearly the elusive and evocative Kaltrina Dahl, who ADVANCES to the very threshold of the PATIO DOOR, where she PAUSES, DRIPPING, and then ENTERS.

METROS (CONT'D)
(stunned, to say the least)
Kaltrina?

KALTRINA DAHL
(dripping, shining, emanating beauty; in a
word, gorgeous)
Yes, Joseph. I've been waiting a long time for you to
find me.

METROS
(overwhelmed)
I ... I ... I feel like I've been waiting a lifetime ...

KALTRINA DAHL
(compelling)
Do you have something you want to ask me, Joseph?

METROS
(striving heroically for Zilch)
Kaltrina, I must implore you to reconsider your separation
from Zero Vaynilovich. I really think he might die! Are
you aware of his predicament?

KALTRINA DAHL
Oh, yes, Joseph. It is likely to be so.

METROS
(urgently entreating)
Then you must go to him at the Queen of Angels Hospital,
before it's too late!

KALTRINA DAHL
I have already made my rounds at all the hospitals of Los
Angeles, including the Children's Hospital -- the angels
are always so innocent there.

METROS
Then you did, or you will, go to see Zilch?

KALTRINA DAHL

I'm sorry, Joseph. That's not possible. Zero, you see, has become enamored -- and unfortunately, not with me. He has become enamored with his style, his words, his techniques, and his personal renown. I'm afraid that such tragic situations are inevitably terminal.

METROS

Is there nothing I can say in his behalf to make you change your mind?

KALTRINA DAHL

Unfortunately, no. My sisters and I are nothing if not selective.
        (dripping with sympathy)
But you might consider offering me something of your own accord …
        (like a repetition of a riddle)
Do you have something you want to ask me, Joseph?

METROS

        (appears dizzy, confused)
I … I think so, but I'm afraid.

KALTRINA DAHL

        (her voice becoming louder, reverberating,
        and then fading)
Unvarnished fear is just the beginning of wisdom …
Joseph … Joseph …

CLOSE ON - Kaltrina's heavenly FACE - As she speaks, she gently SMILES at Metros, who stares expressionless, with unseeing eyes, trembling, suddenly young and foolish.

As her resonant words (REVERB) fade out; the SCENE FADES/ TRANSITIONS TO:

BEGIN METROS'S FLASHBACK to a fear-laced DANCE SCENE of his PRETEEN PAST: A YOUNG BOY, awkward, reluctant -- before the heat of the rut -- STANDS ACROSS the DANCE FLOOR from a beautiful GIRL-CHILD; He STANDS FROZEN, with a child's heart.

> KALTRINA DAHL'S VOICE (O.S.)
> (gentle Reverb narration)
> Do you have something you want to ask me, Joseph?

The YOUNG METROS looks down at his shoes, nervously attending the hanging shard of a thumbnail.

> METROS (O.S.)
> (his child's heart speaking through Dr. Metros's voice)
> Yes, I do, but I need your help. All I can see are those eyes that belong to heaven. All I can feel is the warmth of that smile that carries me away.

We see the beautiful GIRL-CHILD LOOKING at YOUNG METROS across the DANCE FLOOR.

> KALTRINA DAHL'S VOICE (O.S.)
> And who do you think inspires the child to span the vast distances of desire? Who do you think inspires the man to take those first bold steps into an even greater unknown?

The reluctant YOUNG METROS takes his first ambivalent STEPS ...

> METROS (O.S.)
> Yes, I remember. They were awkward steps. They were tremulous steps.

> KALTRINA DAHL'S VOICE (O.S.)
> Awkward, yes, tremulous, yes ... but to me, they were always endearing. Don't you remember what it is you asked me? It was very nearly, but not exactly, like a prayer ...

The YOUNG BOY approaches the beautiful GIRL-CHILD …

                    METROS (O.S.)
Yes, I remember now. It was more like a moment, in the
loneliest of moments, in the most compelling of moments,
when you <u>dare to reach out</u> …

              KALTRINA DAHL'S VOICE (O.S.)
Now that you remember … Do you have something you
want to ask me, Joseph?

The YOUNG BOY and the GIRL-CHILD are standing FACE-TO-FACE.

                    METROS (O.S.)
Yes, Kaltrina, there surely is. I would … I would … <u>I would
love</u> …

                                        <u>END FLASHBACK.</u>

ACTION: There is a MONTAGE OF IMAGES -- a PASSIONATE
EMBRACE, the brink of a SUNRISE, a bevy of SWANS IN FLIGHT, as
the MUSIC RISES. <u>SMASH CUT - BACK TO THE PRESENT</u>: ANGLE
ON - METROS: a full-grown philosopher, who for the love of wisdom,
REACHES OUT with both his arms to EMBRACE the eternal beauty
before him (KALTRINA), HOLDING ON tightly with his heart on his
sleeve.

AT THIS VERY MOMENT, Manifesta, delayed, perhaps, by an extended
number of appreciative encores at the Hollywood Bowl, ARRIVES BACK
HOME.

                    MANIFESTA
           (stares accusingly; notices that Metros's shirt
           and pants are clearly <u>soaking wet</u>)
You men are so damned predictable! I believe I even
warned you about this!

Metros hesitates to respond, given the soggy situation and the inherent ponderousness of any conceivable explanation.

> KALTRINA DAHL
> (unfazed, in her normal voice)
> Welcome home, Mani dear. Did Ludwig van Beethoven manage to roll over during the performance, as you planned?

> MANIFESTA
> (piqued yet dignified)
> I had the old boy doing backflips.

The Camera PANS the UNCONVENTIONAL TRIANGLE, set in the most modern of settings:

> NARRATOR, METROS (V.O.)
> There I was, the philosophical counselor, reduced from the august regality of his scholarly profession to a child caught with his hand in the proverbial cookie jar. Kaltrina Dahl, completely comfortable with her near-nakedness, stood gracefully poised with the unruffled radiance of a prima ballerina. Manifesta stood defiant, dressed in a formal conductor's tuxedo, which did nothing to hide the flaming femininity that issued from every crease.

> MANIFESTA
> (with strained civility)
> Kaltrina, may I see you for a moment in private?

> KALTRINA DAHL
> Of course you can, Mani dear.

They LEAVE Metros alone in the room. Metros WANDERS OUT to the POOL AREA, SWITCHES OFF the LIGHT, gazes out at the COAST in the misty MOONLIGHT, and listens to the WIND in the TREES.

SOUNDS of an ARGUMENT are heard, heavily punctuated with occasional HARSH TONES; after a while, SILENCE returns: the WIND in the TREES. Manifesta joins Metros at the RAILING:

MANIFESTA
You'll have to excuse me, Dr. Metropolis. Apparently, jealousy comes with the territory.

METROS
(notices the lucent tearstains on her hyper-feminine cheeks)
I'm sorry if I caused you any --

MANIFESTA
(cutting him off)
Oh, it's not entirely your fault. Muses are nothing if not promiscuous ... and Kaltrina is no exception.
(looking into the distance)
It's just that it annoys me no end when I think ... when I realize that my work is just beginning.
(impassioned, she turns, leans back against the railing)
When I think of all the time and effort I put into this relationship -- all the personal sacrifices she demanded of me -- all the mindless adoration -- all the attention to each and every detail of her instructions, however counterintuitive, however quaint, however precious, it makes me furious!

Metros marvels at the amazing sight: SUBJECTIVE POV - Manifesta LEANING BACK on a RAILING (overlooking the seashore and the city lights); she STANDS DEFIANT, her dark hair tousled by the cool evening breezes, her tearstained cheeks faintly illuminated by the soft light of the moon.

MANIFESTA (CONT'D)
(rising to a climax)
After all, it was <u>my brain</u>, <u>my mind</u>, <u>my</u> heart on the anvil!
It was <u>my will that was forged, above all</u>! How dare she
turn her face to another! How dare she! How dare she turn
that beatific face from me! <u>From me</u>!

Suddenly, we hear the harsh sounds of DOORS SLAMMING loudly in
the BACKGROUND. A grief-stricken Manifesta REACHES FOR and
TOUCHES her EMPTY (sans monocle) tearstained EYE SOCKET. We
hear the SOUND of ONE FINAL DOOR SLAMMING, with a single
THUNDEROUS CLAP!

INT. METROS'S OUTER OFFICE - EARLY EVENING

Metros ENTERS in silence. Holly LOOKS UP expectantly from her
CELEBRITY MAGAZINE. Metros only SHAKES HIS HEAD, SITS
DOWN briefly in a RECEPTION CHAIR to catch his breath, then he
walks over to the WINDOW, opens the curtain, stares out.

METROS
(turns, holds up the keys)
I meant to give these back to you yesterday.

HOLLY
(thumbing through magazine)
Keep 'em, Doc. The Repo Man called and said you could
repossess the Ferrari for a few more days.
(looks up)
But with all your treks up and down the hill to the hospital,
you must be in pretty good shape by now.

METROS
(staring out the window)
Really? I hadn't noticed. Has it been that long?

HOLLY

The accident was more than a week ago. Isn't your favorite client any better?

METROS

Not really, despite the best that modern medicine has to offer -- Zilch is clearly no better. Every day he wakes up with a glimmer of a promise of her return, only to watch it slip away as the days pass, one into another. You know, Holly, I'm beginning to wonder: just how much suffering can a tragic hero be expected to endure?

HOLLY
(sympathetically)
From where I sit, it looks like you're the one who is suffering, right along with your client.

METROS
(nods, continues staring)
I visit his hospital room every day, helpless -- watching him fade away.

HOLLY
(picking up the magazine)
Try to cheer up, Doc. You do a lot of good in this town. At least you try to. I was just reading this article about Manifesta -- Ya know, she's a real success story: It says here she solved "The Whole Equation of Pictures" -- she just got the green light from another motion picture studio ...
(thumbing through the pages)
It says here in the interview that she no longer supports indie productions. When asked about her previous use of nonsanctioned actresses, she says:
(reading)
"There were too many problems with psychological and medical issues involving human resources. I solved these problems, more conveniently, by joining rather than beating all the dead horses."

METROS

Really? Manifesta may have mastered "The Whole Equation of Pictures." But I, for one, liked her better when she was the flaming and the flammable provocateur in love.

HOLLY

(joins Metros at the window)
Speaking about love, Doc. Any news about Scarlett?

METROS

(turns around, wistfully)
Yeah. But nothing worth mentioning ...

HOLLY

(inquisitively)
Well? What's the scoop? Out with it, Doc.

METROS

I haven't seen her. I just heard something. I've been distracted.

HOLLY

(impatiently, pushes him)
No, Doc. You've been avoiding the issue! Tell me about Scarlett ... What did you hear about Scarlett?

METROS

If you must know ... Scarlett has, apparently, become disillusioned with the diminishing returns of her acting career. But she hasn't given up her method acting entirely -- she is currently pretending to be a waitress at a nightclub on the Sunset Strip.

Metros TURNS AWAY and leans his head directly against the glass of the window and sobs. We can almost feel the pain.

HOLLY
(grabs his arm and turns him)
You've got to snap out of it, Doc. I've never seen you so
sad ... It's not healthy!

METROS
I can't help it, Holly. I feel that I've failed my most
important client somehow ... I feel that I could have ...
that I should have done more.

HOLLY
C'mon, Doc. It's not the worst thing that could happen,
you know.

METROS
(grabs Holly's shoulders)
But it is the worst thing, Holly! What if Zilch actually dies
without knowing?

HOLLY
(removes his hands from her shoulders and
steps back)
Without knowing what? What could be so important that
you must suffer along with him?

METROS
(starts pacing)
I find myself thinking, indeed expecting, that philosophy
could be raised once again to a more creative level! By
restoring the flame of wonder to the human mind, it could
provide a guiding light! Like great poetry once did! as
great literature once did! As great works of art once did!
(catching himself; puts his hand over his
mouth for a few beats)
Hold on! Perhaps this is just a fading remnant ... Perhaps
this is what I get for rubbing up against the likes of Kaltrina
Dahl!

HOLLY

Just what kind of "rubbing up" are we talking about here, Doc?

METROS

Forget it, Holly. It's beside the point! I need to do something, and yet I don't know what to do … or even say!

HOLLY

(seats herself on the desk, impatiently wagging
a leg)
Try focusing on what you've learned?

METROS

(pacing, rambling)
Some of the flaws are clear to me: the grandiose persona, the intolerable hubris, the supreme self-assurance of an Apollo who transcends the mundane world … That aspiring impulse, fanned by the flames of Dionysian ecstasy, it brings forth the apex of artistic creativity … That is, until it all falls apart, and degenerates, and ultimately goes under …

HOLLY

Slow down, Doc. You're making me dizzy.

METROS

(standing still)
Is life a dirty trick? Does it favor the most deserving? Honestly, Holly, it's a problem of epic proportions! Still, all I can see from my clinical point of view is the pathos, the drama, and the sadness.

HOLLY

(picks up and reads the case file folder)
In other words, you still have no idea how you're going to solve this case: "The Lost Love of the Latest Tycoon."

METROS
(sits down, dejected)
I'm afraid you might be right.

Just then, a PHONE RINGS: Holly REACHES to answer it. Holly LISTENS. Metros STANDS, looks anxious, realizing that this might be the phone call that he dreaded the most.

HOLLY
(hangs up the phone)
You gotta go, Doc. It sounds like this could be the beginning of the end.

INT. QUEEN OF ANGELS - WAITING ROOM - NIGHT

Metros SITS ALONE in the WAITING ROOM. The ambience of the NIGHT SHIFT creates a disconcerting neo-noir-like setting. An ORDERLY approaches; Metros LOOKS UP; we follow them into THE ROOM. Zilch is in the BED, propped up by pillows, surrounded by low-key lighting and the silence of the NURSING STAFF.

ZILCH
(opens his eyes)
What more should I have offered my misplaced love?

METROS
(to a dying Zilch)
I have no words of my own.

ZILCH
(continues slowly)
How low should I have bowed down before my elusive Blue Dahlia, the exalted eidolon who haunts my dreams?

METROS
(disarmed by the eloquence, he searches hard
for truth)
It is my impression that all she wanted from you was <u>that</u>
<u>which you had yet to give the world, nothing more.</u>

ZILCH
(waxing sadly lyrical)
Should I have come before her with burned offerings, with
a herd of sacrificial calves? Would she have been more
pleased with the gift of a hundred handsome actors or a
thousand derricks pumping oil? Should I have offered up
my admiring audiences for my prideful transgressions,
the fruit of all my labors for the sins of my soul? Did she
truly expect that my admiring audiences would be born
posthumously?

METROS
(sympathetically, moving closer to the side of
Zilch's bed)
I think you already know what she tried to teach you, Mr.
Zilch. I think you already know what she considered to be
the greatest good.

ZILCH
(weakly, looking to Metros)
Tell me anyway, in case I missed it.

METROS
She wanted you to <u>think justly</u> and to appreciate the
meaning of humility and compassion, which she -- above
all -- embodies in her endless love of man.

ZILCH
(finally, sincerely)
Can you please speak more clearly, Metropolis? My
hearing, as well as my eyesight, seems to be fading from me.

                    METROS
        (leaning closer into the shadowy chiaroscuro
         of Zilch's face, speaks slowly, clearly)
      I think she just wanted you to walk humbly by her side …
      to walk with her again in the presence of the divine.

                    ZILCH
      Oh, is that all?

                    METROS
      Yes, I think it is.

                    ZILCH
        (as if struggling for breath)
      There must be more! Tell me why, Mr. Philosopher. Tell me
      why my love was not strong enough to hold her!

Metros LOOKS UP, as though he were searching for answers in a world
above and beyond our world. LAP DISSOLVE - to PHANTOM POV:
Looking DOWN at the BED SCENE. ANGLE ON - Zilch, with Metros
close beside him. CLOSER ON - Metros KNEELING DOWN.

                    METROS
        (pastoral tonality, with emphatic caesuras)
      Her love for you was not meant to last … It was meant to
      shine … It was meant to shine through you.

Metros looks more closely at Zilch; he sees that the lights of his pale gray
EYES are already DIM, and the BREATH of his tortured soul has finally
let go of its inspiration. Greatly alarmed, Metros LOOKS UP at the solemn
NURSES in attendance.

                    METROS (CONT'D)
        (loudly, frantically)
      Did he hear me?
        (louder, "echoing")
      Did he even hear me?

EXT. HOSPITAL TO OFFICE - METROS WALKS IN DESPAIR - NIGHT

Metro WALKS from the Queen of Angels Hospital, CROSSES the intersection at Hollywood and Sunset. ANGLE ON - the VISTA THEATER, Marquis reads, "Coming Soon: Much Ado About Nada"; we see SOMBER PEOPLE exiting the antiquated theater, as though leaving a funeral wake. CLOSER ON - PASSERSBY: Metros encounters a series of ACCUSATORY EYES. Various STREET PEOPLE appear to GLARE at Metros as he makes his way to his OFFICE.

> NARRATOR, METROS (V.O.)
> It had to end. I knew that from the beginning. But knowing something beforehand is no consolation; not when your last remaining client is moved from death row to the gallows of endless time, leaving you, his philosophical counselor, languishing on the chain of your own failed expectations.
> (walking faster to avoid the seemingly accusatory stares)
> Knowing something is no consolation when your latest client is as dead as ancient history and your love life is washed up on a deserted beach like a gutless abalone shell -- a shell that is devoid of all meaning, save for the emptiness and despair -- a shell with a hole in it large enough for a certain dame to put her fist right through.

Metros passes street people, noticing the accusatory eyes.

> NARRATOR, METROS (V.O.) (CONT'D)
> Even complete strangers know the score in this sad city; they follow you with their eyes blinking, hissing at you like angry cats. Eyes squinting like stilettos at your every step ... eyes evading you like the trailing tones of a police siren that veers off in another direction ...
> (The SIREN fades; Metros passes a shadowy person who watches)
> Even worse, there are eyes that continue to stare at you with an expressionless silence that speaks to you of your

failures with relentless disapproval, if not with complete contempt. Some nights have a thousand of those eyes!

ANGLE ON - CITY LIGHTS in "Bokeh" focus. Metros reaches his OFFICE; a metal GATE OPENS; he ENTERS the relative DARKNESS of the PARKING GARAGE; he REAPPEARS in the topless FERRARI.

MATCH-CUT DRIVE SCENES: We see Metros DRIVING HARD - merging onto Interstate 5, speeding past Dodger Stadium, arching onto the 110 Pasadena Freeway, winding along the historic Arroyo Seco Parkway, then SLOWING DOWN dramatically and motoring SLOWLY along the antique-lamplit Millionaires Mile of Orange Grove Boulevard, Pasadena, up to the BARRICADES that block the entrance of the notorious SUICIDE BRIDGE.

> NARRATOR, METROS (V.O.) (CONT'D)
> On a night like this, when you know you can't sleep, you can always drive … You can drive hard, and with all possible speed … because driving is like forgetting … and driving makes you concentrate … just to stay alive … and driving somehow makes everything possible again … it allows you to believe again … it allows you to believe that you can leave those thousand eyes far behind …

EXT. PASADENA/COLORADO STREET - SUICIDE BRIDGE - NIGHT

We FOCUS ON - Metros DRIVING UP to an imposing barrier: a huge wood-plank GATE of a Highway BARRICADE; the SIGN reads "Route 66 - ROAD CLOSED." Metros gets out to investigate. He PUSHES and PUSHES against the GATE, to no avail. He TURNS around, with his back to the GATE/SIGN, and continues V.O., illuminated by the headlights of the FERRARI.

> METROS (V.O.) (CONT'D)
> First you dream, and then you die. It's the title of an unfinished story of a life. My life certainly. Perhaps even yours …

Metros SPINS around again and PUSHES, harder this time; he THROWS his shoulder into the effort, painfully, again and again until he is battered and exhausted. He RAISES HIS FISTS into the air as he CIRCLES around, SHOUTING OUT LOUD.

> METROS
> (exasperated and enraged)
> Oh, what a miserable failure am I! A philosophical counselor who can't save his client! ... Who can't save his lover! ... Who can't even make his way onto the Pasadena Suicide Bridge!

Metros BEATS his FISTS on the "Road Closed" SIGN until he falls to the ground in a ruinous state.

Slowly, amazingly, the massive DOORS of the wood-plank GATE OPEN to the inside, clearing the path to the SUICIDE BRIDGE. Metros STANDS UP, DRIVES the FERRARI slowly onto the curved roadway of the Beaux-Arts BRIDGE; he STOPS midway, leaves the HEADLIGHTS ON, STEPS OVER the guard RAILING to the SIDEWALK.

Metros CLIMBS UP HIGH into a raised ALCOVE flanked by two antique LAMPPOSTS -- large glass balls glowing faintly, like ill-illumined grapes, create an aura of theatricality. We see the ghostly cliffside Vista Del Arroyo Hotel in the background. ANGLE ON - Metros, who is LEANING OUT, REACHING dangerously into darkness, quite possibly to end it all ...

> WOMAN'S VOICE (O.S.)
> (it's actually Darla Darkcity)
> So, you're the one who is charged with addressing one of the world's oldest and most deeply disturbing woes ... I've never met anyone who could even dream of doing such a thing!

ANGLE ON (METROS'S POV) - we see DARLA DARKCITY, lying seductively on the HOOD of the FERRARI, lights still on.

METROS
(looking down from his perch on the suicide
prevention rails)
Darla Darkcity! In the flesh, no less! I must say, you're very
lovely for a mental hallucination!

DARLA DARKCITY
(sits up, flourishes her hair)
Oh, you're a smart one! Like a knight on a chessboard
who can move nimbly up and over prickly hurdles,
surmounting obstacles that would be impossible for other
lesser players to leap over.

METROS
(increasingly impatient)
The major problem with your analogy is that philosophy
is not a game for knights! The other problem with your
analogy is that you're not even real! It doesn't matter what
I think or do; I just turn around and you're gone … as in
gone … and I'm still here dangling, on my own suicide
watch!

Metros TURNS back and around, and indeed DARLA DARKCITY has
disappeared, leaving only the FERRARI and its headlights.

METROS (CONT'D)
(turns back, reaches far out, then stops, turns,
reflects)
Just what I thought. It's a bitter little world, but I wouldn't
want to drown it with my philosophy.

WOMAN'S VOICE (O.S.)
(soft, cool, resonant, the voice of Kaltrina Dahl)
It is that urbane humility of yours that makes you so
useful, Joseph. It is the very thing that qualifies you for
this philosophical road you are on.

Metros LOOKS DOWN at the ROAD; he LOOKS over to the FERRARI, and finding it barren, HE TURNS farther, and finally, he finds the figure of KALTRINA DAHL standing nearly naked (in a sheer, semitransparent, formfitting halter dress), standing there in the theatrical fog, illuminated by the gauzy stage lights of the Ferrari.

METROS

(dramatically, overwrought)
Kaltrina Dahl! The elusive Blue Dahlia. How luminous of you to come! I was half expecting the Spider-Woman. By the way, you just missed my previous visitation -- she was very convincing! Tell me -- how does this work?
(pointing to the lamp globes)
Is it like these manifold glow-bulbs here? Are you all one and the same -- a goddess with a dozen faces?

KALTRINA DAHL

(her voice is soft and cool, her eyes clear and bright)
It is very nearly, but not exactly, like that, Joseph. But my sisters and I are nothing if not discrete.

METROS

(philosophically distraught)
Because that would explain a lot! Let me see -- Venus, Sophia, the Charities, Muses, Graces: Which one is it tonight?

KALTRINA DAHL

(reaching out to poor Metros)
You don't have to <u>name us</u> to <u>know us</u>, Joseph.

Metros is inescapably drawn to the luminous beauty, as before. He CLIMBS DOWN from the pointed iron bars of the Suicide Bridge. He crosses the sidewalk, steps over the guardrail, and STANDS TREMBLING at the edge of the pavement.

KALTRINA DAHL (CONT'D)
On this stage of life that is arrayed before you, Joseph,
shouldn't you consider the possibilities -- the intellectual,
the philosophical, the dramatic possibilities -- of one more
dance with me?

METROS
(a moment of hesitation, a moment of
remembrance, and then acceptance)
I will ... I do ... I cherish even the thought!

A climactic CRESCENDO of tasteful MUSIC accompanies the ACTION
(captured by a 360-degree PAN MOVE) as Metros JOINS Kaltrina and they
begin to DANCE in the misty haze of the elevated roadway.

In the confusion of emotion and the fog of mental distress, a number of
other LUMINOUS FIGURES seem to APPEAR for a brief and shining
moment, only to EVAPORATE as the MUSIC FADES, leaving Metros alone
with Kaltrina in his arms. Kaltrina SMILES at Metros, DISENGAGES, and
then TURNS to leave.

METROS (CONT'D)
(with newfound desperation)
Kaltrina, don't go!

KALTRINA DAHL
My sisters and I are rapidly disappearing from this modern
world, as you can see at the very edge of night. You know
we are well beyond the pale of an endangered species,
Joseph. We are very nearly, but not exactly, extinct.

METROS
(holding out his arms)
"Very nearly, but not exactly" -- I remember clearly now. Is
there nothing I can say or do to convince you to stay with
me a little while longer?

KALTRINA DAHL
(simply smiles divinely and places her finger
to her lips)
Shhhh!

METROS
(reluctant yet accepting)
You mean it would be best for me to love you from afar …
as I love wisdom, as I love beauty and truth?

Hearing these words, Kaltrina returns to EMBRACE the humble
philosopher; a long, lavish, EXCEEDINGLY PASSIONATE KISS attends
a FULL BODY ENVELOPMENT, which proceeds with such moving,
pleasing, sensuous insinuations that one hesitates to put mere pen to paper,
leaving instead the unchaste stir of voluptuous beauty in the innocent mind
(eye) of the beholder.

Kaltrina STARTS TO LEAVE. Metros HOLDS ON TO HER HAND tightly,
reluctant to let her go.

METROS (CONT'D)
(pleading, as never before)
Kaltrina! Please! I'm not ready to continue on without
your blessed inspiration. I know for certain that I can no
longer do it alone!

KALTRINA DAHL
(sweetly, profoundly)
Dear Joseph Metropolis, my woebegone philosopher to the
stars … my hero who seeks to save all the lost angels …
isn't it time for you to realize … it's enough for me that
you try?

Kaltrina's HEAVENLY SMILE stills any protests. She KISSES Metros on
the LIPS one last time, PRESSES SOMETHING firmly into his HAND, and
WHISPERS softly into his EAR.

KALTRINA DAHL (CONT'D)
(whispering succinctly)
You don't have to do it alone, Joseph. You might consider taking Scarlett to the ballet sometime soon. Even the darkest of damsels and swans can have their romantic compensations.

Kaltrina TURNS and LEAVES (i.e., Fades Out); Metros HESITATES and then TURNS AROUND and WALKS in the illuminated fog toward the dual headlights of the FERRARI.

Metros SADDLES UP to the "Prancing Horse" and DRIVES FORWARD: forward into the emptiness of the vacant Beaux-Arts Bridge ... forward into the fog of the future ... forward into life.

NARRATOR, METROS (V.O.)
(slowly approaching the FERRARI)
Although it is terribly hard for a man to let go of such a wondrous and enchanting dream of beauty, there could be no finer choice. I saddled up to the Prancing Horse and began to drive forward: forward into the emptiness of the Beaux-Arts Bridge ... forward into the fog of the future ... forward into life.
(driving forward into the fog)
I didn't have to look to know what gift Kaltrina Dahl had placed into my hand. Some mysteries need not be solved with such <u>exactness</u>. Like all great gifts, you can assume that it is fragile and precious and fleeting, like life itself. My life certainly, perhaps even yours.
(driving farther away on the bridge)
I couldn't help thinking about Scarlett that night -- thinking a lot about the unpleasantness of her history. But mostly, I was thinking about that smile -- that smile she smiles just for me. Who knows? Maybe I'll give her a call.

FADE OUT.

<u>THE END</u>

ACKNOWLEDGMENTS

The author would like to thank his friends and colleagues in the movie business whose generous assistance, encouragement, comments, recommendations, and script notes served to improve both the form and the content of this screenplay. With special thanks to Eugene Kelly, Phillip Eckhardt, and Tyler Van Patten.

TRUE DIRECTIONS
An affiliate of Tarcher Books

OUR MISSION

Tarcher's mission has always been to publish books
that contain great ideas. Why? Because:

GREAT LIVES BEGIN WITH GREAT IDEAS

At Tarcher, we recognize that many talented authors, speakers,
educators, and thought-leaders share this mission and deserve to be
published – many more than Tarcher can reasonably publish ourselves.
True Directions is ideal for authors and books that increase awareness,
raise consciousness, and inspire others to live their ideals and passions.

Like Tarcher, True Directions books are designed to do three things:
inspire, inform, and motivate.

Thus, True Directions is an ideal way for these important voices to
bring their messages of hope, healing, and help to the world.

Every book published by True Directions– whether it is non-fiction, memoir,
novel, poetry or children's book – continues Tarcher's mission to publish works
that bring positive change in the world. We invite you to join our mission.

For more information, see the True Directions website:
www.iUniverse.com/TrueDirections/SignUp

Be a part of Tarcher's community to bring positive change in this world!
See exclusive author videos, discover new and exciting books, learn about
upcoming events, connect with author blogs and websites, and more!
www.tarcherbooks.com

TRUE DIRECTIONS
AN AFFILIATE OF TARCHER BOOKS

Printed in the United States
By Bookmasters